Family Reunions

Clan Gatherings

by
Shari L. Fiock

OTHER WORKS
designed, illustrated, or compiled
by
Shari Fiock

SHARI AND ASSOCIATES   1974-
Design Entrepreneur: Public Relations& Advertising
Desktop Publishing, Displays and Dioramas
    KLAMATH NATIONAL FOREST   1979 -
    Interpretive Museum, Research, Displays and Dioramas
    CASCADE WORLD FOUR SEASON RESORT   1980 -
    Writer, Public Relations Consultant
    Richard M. Cowardin, Developer
    TEACHERS INTRODUCTION & PLANNING GUIDE
    TO TEACHING THE ART OF INVENTING   1990
    Illustrated and typeset the book, etc.
    (Honorable Mention - National Writers Club-Contest)
    Maggie Weisberg and Mel Fuller, Authors
    TOP O'THE STATE DISTRICT
    CALIFORNIA GARDEN CLUB'S, INC.   1990
    Illustrated and typeset their annual book
    Dudley Zoller, Director
    AGRI-EDUCATION 2000   1989
    Illustrated and typeset all material
    Mimi Van Sickle, coordinator
    WILDLAND FIRES   1986
    Illustrated the book
    Lee Morford, author
    HOLIDAY FUN BOOK   1978
    FLIGHTS OF FANCY   1989
    Illustrated the books
    Lou Sharon, author

ARTRE ENTERPRISES (store fixture company)   **1968-1974**
Co-owner/ designer

OREGON HOLIDAYS (Monthly magazine)   *1966-1969*
Staff artist
    . BEAVER officially proclaimed Oregon state animal
    Researcher and developer of Oregon state souvenir
    etal per Governor McCall

NATIONAL WRITERS CLUB   *1991 -*
Pacific Northwest Representative

WHO'S WHO OF AMERICAN WOMEN   *1987 -*

Ed: Art Instruction Schools, Inc: Advertising and Related Arts 1964

FAMILY LIFE

Family Reunions

CLAN GATHERINGS

How-to assemble a memorable event for clan gatherings.
(clan, Klan, n. (Gael, and Ir. clann, family, tribe))
A group of related persons;
a body of persons closely united by some common interest or pursuit.

by
Shari L. Fiock

©Coyote Publishing

Yreka, CA 96097 - 1854

FAMILY REUNIONS AND CLAN GATHERINGS

Published by
Coyote Publishing
Yreka, California 96097-1854

Printed by
McNaughton and Gunn Lithographers

Photography Credits
Barbara Hull: Sample A, Meamber Family Tree
Bill Schmidt: Sample B, Fiock Family Tree

Poem Illustration
Sterling C. Fiock

Illustrations and Cover Art
Shari L. Fiock

Library of Congress Cataloging-in Publication
Library of Congress Catalog Card Number 91-71053
ISBN 0-9628801-0-8

CONTENTS

FAMILY REUNIONS AND CLAN GATHERINGS

FORMS, CHARTS and SAMPLES

PHOTOGRAPHS

GROUP RECIPES

FAMILY REUNIONS AND CLAN GATHERINGS

Acknowledgments:

My father, Webster, and son, Sterling,
for their love, patience, and unwavering support;

Edwinna (Lou) Sharon,
Margaret Alderman,
Julia Allen,
and
Alan Sleep,
proof-reading team;

Everyone who share the enthusiasm of having a supportive family unit, and active extended families, expecially:

CleoAntoine, Linda (Grein) Barcus, Jone Carlson, Jan Cozzalio, Jan Cowardin, Thelma Davis, Jim Ellis, Debbie Fiock, Evelyn (Runnels) Fiock, Frey Family, Lois & Grant Gibson, Gundlach-Poirot Family, Dr. Ernest Hayes, Deb-E Herrera, Monica Hall, Anne Hughes, Barbara Hull, Robbie Hutchison, Carole Koch, Meamber Family, Erma Lee Minton, Ev Morris, Jim Norland, Lori Potter and the McNaughton & Gunn artisans, Bishop Stephen Probst, Merle Pruett, Raul Family, Donvan Rogers, Bill Schmidt, Mary Simmons, Smith Family, Yvonne Steinbring, Barbara Taylor, Trammel Family, Jim Walker, Zelma Walter, Annette Wetherington, Mary Zubricky, a very special group for their continual and valued 'anonymous' contributions, and many others for their valuable input and encouragement in preparing this publication to help families everywhere enjoy...

FAMILY REUNIONS AND CLAN GATHERINGS.

FAMILY REUNIONS AND CLAN GATHERINGS

FAMILY LIFE

If you could see your ancestors
All standing in a row
Would you be proud of them or not
Or don't you really know?
Some strange discoveries are made
In climbing family trees
And some of them I am afraid;
Would not exactly please.

If you could see your ancestors
All standing in a row
There might be some of them perhaps
You would not care to know
But there's another question
Which requires a different view
If you should meet your ancestors
Would they be proud of you?

Author Unknown

Poem discovered by May Fiock during research at the
Library of Congress
Washington D.C., U.S.A.

FAMILY LIFE

Introduction

Perhaps as a child you had a favorite uncle who took you fishing, a grand-parent who smothered you in hugs and kisses, always knowing your endeavors were exceptional.
When was the last time you visited them? Will your children have those memories? Or will their memories be filled with summer camp counselors; an occasional teacher; individuals who recognized their outstanding attributes for a moment in life's time span then are forgotten? Childhood friends, confidants, co-workers and neighbors, for the most part, are like paths that cross or ships that pass in the night and are off to more pressing issues. Indeed, there are exceptions, but that is leaving a child's supportive network system to chance.

During the six years of interviewing organizers of family reunions and clan gatherings I learned they unanimously believe these events help individuals develop life long networks that increase personal worth, confidence and self-esteem in addition to perpetuating the family nucleus.

Dr. Hayes, DMP, summarized this issue when he stated, "In the old days the whole family worked together for the good of the family team. If the years bounty was profitable perhaps they bought a new finagled thing called a washing machine. The whole family would gather around and rejoice in making mom's work easier. It was like the frosting on the cake. It seems to me that too many families today have the frosting without the cake." But we can help put the 'cake' back into our families through reunions. Give your loved ones a nucleus for life, a bonding foundation of support ... the extended family. Many families shared their experiences in Family Reunions and Clan Gatherings to help you make your event a "Thank goodness I came" and not a "Why'd I bother?" memory.

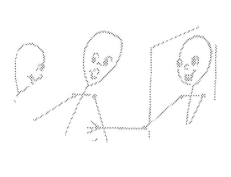

FAMILY REUNIONS & CLAN GATHERINGS

Family, it's a word that conjures entire visions of worlds; sitting on grandpa's lap while grandma takes hot cookies from the oven, uncles and aunts with their children, indeed memories of love and security. It is too important a foundation for your descendants and those of your siblings not to experience. Think how much it means to have the knowledge of the extended family; of all the treasured memories. Give this priceless gift to your loved ones, hold a family reunion in six months to a year from today.

Families in today's society are often restricted to an immediate nucleus of a single parent, perhaps both parents work with one or two children or various combinations of step-relatives. In the late 1800's and early 1900's families, frequently, had six or more children. This gave the child a foundation and parents were more less assured close kinship with at least some grown children and their families. With smaller families in our mobile society, many people are not able to enjoy the benefits of having an active 'extended' family. But we can bring our scattered stress filled lives into better perspective through uniting the clan. So take advantage of our mobility and reach out to the descendants of a mutual progenitor: great-great-great-grandfather, perhaps. Not only will this unite the clan, it'll probably create a network spanning the nation. This can help youngsters understand our nation, possibly expand their knowledge of national and global opportunities.

There is a plethora of information available for organizing family reunions but very little for clan gatherings. (I couldn't find any - so our first clan gathering was processed as a job. Since 1968 I have been self-employed in public relations and advertising, thus I'd organized various activities.) With the success of our first gathering many potential clan organizers asked me how they could organize an event for their family. As word spread other clan organizers throughout the United States contacted me to share their experiences, too.

Involvement is the main factor of a successful event. Determine the progenitor (the starting member of your extended family), many families use a third or fourth great-grand-parent. On a piece of paper note his* descendants, then their descendants and so forth until you reach the generation which has enthusiastic clan gathers. Try to have the organization committee reflect equal representation from the various branches. This will be difficult at best, with health, distance, and interest varying extensively. For the branches that are not represented appoint a proxy, be sure that the members of that branch know their proxy. Now, set a date within a month or two for the first organizational committee meeting. Ask them to bring their family's address file, make a list of ideas

---

[1] "He" is used solely for the purpose of writing clarity. I firmly believe women can and do organize most reunions and clan gatherings.

and suggestions.

With your interest and enthusiasm in clan gatherings you will probably be the coordinator, at least for the first time. If not, the group should select a coordinator, as they fill the vice president, secretary and treasurer positions at the first meeting. If you have a large organization committee appoint a correspondence secretary, and hostess or host. Read the book to understand the various components of organizing a clan gathering.

It costs to organize a clan gathering. Some clan events are started with donated money and time; others maintain expense records with reimbursement to follow. Full reimbursement is recommended as it can increase participation and involvement in future gatherings. A few families had interesting alternatives which are shared elsewhere in the book.

12 WAYS TO EMPOWER OTHERS [2]

Delegation is a tricky task. Too much oversight and you risk alienating your workers by making them feel you don't trust them. Not enough and the project you've delegated could collapse into chaos. But by following this 12-step process developed by Dick Lohr, president of the Institute of Management and Sales Techniques, Inc. of Newport News, you can increase your chances of success. This guide was adapted from Lohr's audio cassette seminar, How to Delegate Work and Ensure It's Done Right, by CareerTrack, Inc. of Boulder.

1. Set a clear and simple objective.

2. Select a delegate. A challenging task may give an average person a chance to shine, so don't automatically choose your

---

[2] "12 WAYS TO EMPOWER OTHERS", Success, June 1988, p.41, and Quill Pen Pal, November 1989.

best worker. Ask for volunteers and you may be surprised by who responds.

3. If necessary, train the delegatee to prepare him for the task. Remember, delegation should build confidence, so select an assignment that will stretch, but not break, the volunteer.

4. When discussing the project, ask for ideas. He may see it in an entirely different light. This also assures that he understands the goals.

5. Assign the task and explain to the person why you've chosen him. This will tell him that you value his judgment and aren't just pushing grunt work his way.

6. Provide needed guidance. This doesn't mean telling the person "how to do it." It means giving him all the facts he needs, suggesting carefully, possible approaches, and describing the expected results.

7. Make a delegation "contract". This establishes how much freedom he will have with the committee resources, how often you'll follow up. In the case of clan gatherings make it fun while stressing the importance of his job.

8. Establish controls, such as budget, and deadline.

9. Maintain control over all aspects of the project. Set up a "tickler file" to remind yourself to check on the progress.

10. Provide comments, whether positive or negative.

11. Evaluate the finished project. Notes made in the tickler file will remind you of what went right and what went wrong.

12. Benefits of delegation; everyone benefits, especially in conjunction with family activities. It makes the project become theirs, which develops pride and makes each one try harder to make the clan gathering or family reunion successful.

   The article continues with the recommendation to identify the lessons you've learned. Perhaps you didn't follow up often enough, so you will be able to correct the situation during the next event you delegate.

OFFICERS AND COMMITTEES OUTLINE

PRESIDENT OR COORDINATOR

Maintains order in uniting the family for a gathering.

Motivates committees to complete assignments timely.

Keeps immediate proceeding reunion's records. Gives past records to the family historian.

VICE PRESIDENT OR SITE COORDINATOR

Resumes presidential duties if necessary.

Selects sites as appropriate.

SECRETARY OR PUBLIC RELATIONS COORDINATOR

Generates enthusiasm before and during the reunion.

Informs family through newsletters, public through press releases.

TREASURER

Pays, records and maintains reunion or clan finances.

Activities

Encourages circulation and mingling activities.

Networks with all committees.

Coordinates sports and other activities.

Gathers brochures and information on local points of interest.

Plans tours for visiting historical family sites, and other points of interest.

Addresses

Gathers addresses and searches for missing relatives.

Prepares address lists as needed.

Beverage

Assures enough and appropriate liquid is available.

Food

Coordinates and arranges meals.

Works closely with site and activity committees.

Genealogy and History

Establishes and maintains a family 'roots' library.

Host/Hostess

Helps out of town members feel welcome.

Master Of Ceremonies/Program

Makes the programs interesting and informative.

Photographer

Family member or professional studio records events visually.

May process the film and distribute prints.

Registration

Records information to facilitate operations during event.

Security

Assures protection for heirlooms on display at reunion.

Signage

Makes signs and other art related items.

Supply

Maintains a list of who has what available, notes if it can be borrowed for the event.

Gathers and returns items timely.

The coordinator keeps committees aware of schedules, deadlines and opportunities. In brief, he sees the project progresses smoothly to a "Thank goodness I came" event. Efforts of this size often become similar to a 'baby', coddled, coaxed and encouraged.

A...C...T don't RE ACT.

Agitators can cause problems. In some instances communicating on a one-to-one basis is the logical choice. In a friendly, optimistic voice inform the individual a democratic, governing board officiates and directs the development of the event. Reinforce the option by stressing the importance of unity, adding that the success of the event depends upon team effort. To 'act', you might assign him to a position that has high visibility, but won't be critically missed if he changes his mind.

Praise efforts.

Recognize chairpersons and committee workers through newsletters, news releases and during the program. Everyone exerts more effort when there is peer recognition. Encourage committee members to complete projects on time; otherwise, it becomes your obligation and responsibility.

Be flexible and understanding. Encourage new ideas. Accept volunteers to chair new and various responsibilities as they are offered. I received a phone call before one of our events asking if he could be in charge of balloons. Sounded great, he put such a spectacular production with the balloons that many people still comment on them some six years later.

Leaders receive condemnation as well as praise. Hold tight to the praise, and evaluate the criticism, if it is valid apply it, if it is vindictive try to forget it. I know, easier said then done, but try - to dwell upon the negative will dampen your enthusiasm which others will quickly pick up and spread.

TIME FRAME CALENDAR

A year or so before the planned event form an executive board: Gather addresses and information on family units. Appoint a president, vice president, secretary and treasurer.

A year before:

Send an intention or announcement newsletter to family members.

Make reservations.

Eleven months before or one month after the initial meeting:

Announce the intention dates, sites, and other available

information.

Six months before :

Signage, food, supply and activity groups should be functioning. If professional photographers and musicians are planned, make appointments. Order specialty items: T-shirts, balloons, items to be customized.

Four months before:

Finalize promotional material. Confirm rental equipment. All committees should be operational. Mail the second newsletter with genealogy forms. Change savings account to checking account.

Eight to six weeks before:

Review all committees, project food costs and place orders. Finalize field trips and tours.

Five weeks before:

Send the final (confirmation/prompting) newsletter.

Day before check list:

Activities:

- ❐ Promotional kits.
- ❐ Games and equipment.
- ❐ Trophies.
- ❐ Entertainment/program.

Beverage:

- ❐ Iced and/or hot beverages easily accessible.

Master of Ceremonies/Program:

- ❐ Program planned.
- ❐ Performing groups know their performance time and are prepared.
- ❐ A/V equipment and other special equipment needs located and approved for use.

Food:

- ❒ Restaurant and other facilities reserved.
- ❒ Traffic patterns arranged for convenience and flow.
- ❒ Chilled foods safe.
- ❒ Hot foods hot.
- ❒ Trash cans convenient and easily accessible.

Genealogy/History

- ❒ Prompt book ready.

Hostess/Host

- ❒ Host families prepared or hosting visiting families.
- ❒ Special equipment borrowed, bought and ready for use.

Registration

- ❒ Index cards of family units complete or information requested.
- ❒ 'Office' set up near event's entrance.

Security

- ❒ Viewing area secured.

Signage

- ❒ Family tree.
- ❒ Visitors roster.
- ❒ Name tags.
- ❒ Location signs.

Site

- ❒ Install location signs and family tree.
- ❒ Mark the parking area.
- ❒ Identify reserved area.
- ❒ Tape down electric cords in traffic areas.

Supply

- ❒ Borrowed items listed and identified so they can be returned to proper owner.
- ❒ Purchased items bought.

    After the event but within two weeks hold a post

committee meeting. Each chairperson should submit a report of their respective jobs. Evaluate comments and discuss options. Record recommendations for next event. Send post newsletters with family address lists. If applicable, send a press release to the appropriate newspapers.

GOAL/PLANNER SHEET

Before we go any further I would like to share with you a great organizing tool I use. Place a large circle in the center of a sheet of paper draw six or more smaller circles around its perimeter. Draw an arrow next to each smaller circle pointing towards the center of the larger circle, repeat the cycle only have the arrow pointing from the larger circle into the center of each smaller circle. At the top of the sheet write down the project name, perhaps its goal beneath it.

In the center of the large circle put the project or central goal, in each of the smaller circles write a function that might represent; food, activities, etc. List what the smaller circles can give towards the project goals. Sometimes you can use the small circles to represent months. I heard of a woman putting herself in the larger circle and placing her respective talents in the smaller circle to chart her goals for personal growth. Whatever, it seems to be an adaptable formula with many uses.

When the project I am working on is complex I have a separate sheet for the various activities needed. One might represent a television ad, another a radio spot, and so forth with the cover sheet showing each separate sheet in the smaller cover sheet circles. Also, in the business I usually use a larger sheet of paper with larger circles so I can write easier, and it is usually horizontal which allows the circles to circle the larger one more equally.

FAMILY LIFE

Name:_____ Date:_____
Goal:_____

SUPPORT

SUPPORT

SUPPORT

PROJECT

SUPPORT

SUPPORT

SUPPORT

FAMILY REUNIONS AND CLAN GATHERINGS

OH! JUST HEARD ANOTHER TIP!

The Genealogical Helper, published by Everton Publishers (P.O. Box 368, Logan, Utah 84321) lists family reunions and organizations in one periodical each year. Dorothy Ansburgey Griffith continues by stating, "County or State Historical Societies may have knowledge of the intended reunion or family organization. Even Chamber of Commerce's may offer assistance on the subject. Regardless of whom you write be sure to enclose a self-addressed-stamped-envelope for an expedited reply."

ARTICLE 1
NAME AND DEFINITION

Section 1. The name of this organization shall be: The (surname of the starting or base family) Family of (resident country, state county or community).

Section 2. The (surname) family of (Country, state, county and town, if possible) is an association of descendants of (maternal given name) and (paternal given name) uniting to benefit the family through (fellowship appears as a common denominator; however, some families unite for a specific goal).

ARTICLE II
OBJECTS AND PURPOSE

Section 1. The (Surname) family objectives shall be: (a) to establish and maintain communication with the descendants of (maternal and paternal given names); (b) to develop a spirit of friendship and unity among the family; (c) to contribute to the genealogical file; (d) to (your specific family objectives and purposes).

ARTICLE III
MEMBERSHIP

Section 1. All descendants of (maternal and paternal given

names[3]): (a) his present spouse; (b) his x-spouse; (c) his widower; (d) his adopted family members; (e) his step-children; (f) his family's special consideration.

ARTICLE IV
OFFICERS

Section 1. Officers shall be:

President, Vice President, Secretary, Treasurer and Immediate Past President.

Other officers as needed(for your specific family).

Section 2. Term consists of (number) years between reunions.

Section 3. The president shall: (a) preside at meetings and the events; (b) direct the conduct of the business activities, acting as its chief officer; (c) call the meeting to order; (d) approve the agenda for meeting and reunion program; (e) conduct (your specific activity).

Section 4. The vice president shall: (a) assist the president as requested; (b) act as president when the latter is unable; (c) establish site locations for the reunion; (d) perform other functions as needed.

Section 5. The secretary shall: (a) keep minutes of all meetings of the executive board and act as secretary at the reunion meeting; (b) direct the issuance of calls to and the agenda of the meetings and reunions; (c) provide an independent report of all meetings of the executive board and arrange for the permanent retention of past records; (d) conduct (as needed for your family).

Section 6. The treasurer shall: (a) supervise the financial transactions of the family organization; (b) collect and disperse the (surname) Family dues; (c) conduct (responsibilities

---

[3] Today's society has become so entangled that guidelines must be established early. Use a formula applicable to your situation and family.

requested by the executive board

Section 7. Any permanent vacancy in an office shall be filled by the executive board as nominated or submitted by the family members in good standing with their annual dues.

ARTICLE V

ELIGIBILITY FOR OFFICE

Section 1. Be a member of (surname) Family and; (a) be current with dues; (b) (your criteria).

ARTICLE VI

NOMINATIONS AND ELECTIONS

Section 1. The nominations and elections shall take place during or after each reunion.

Section 2. Voting by current paid dues' members only.

Section 3. Nominees must be current with their dues.

Section 4. Election to be by secret ballot/hand/voice and (percentage) majority shall elect the officer.

Section 5. Installation shall be during the last segment of the reunion so the (surname) Family know the officers in charge of the next reunion.

Section 6. In the event of an emergency nominations may be prepared by the executive board and presented as a slate to the family for approval.

Section 7. (your requirements)

ARTICLE VII

AMENDMENTS

Section 1. This constitution may be amended by an affirmative vote of the majority of the board members provided: (a) that the amendment has been proposed by a dues paying member of good standing or by a committee chairperson; (b) (protective measurers appropriate for your specific family).

Section 2. Unless otherwise provided by the executive board before the adoption of an amendment or in a motion to adopt it, amendments to the constitution shall take effect at the close of the meeting at which they were adopted unless otherwise stipulated.

Customize the constitution to fit your requirements. Events flow better when there is an outline of procedures drafted before confrontation. Robert's Rule of Procedures book is an excellent guide to follow for organizations although too restrictive for numerous families who prefer a more casual format.

When, Where and Who

When is the best time for your family to get together?
Some predominantly retired or professional families prefer
winter months when lodging, and many tourist attraction rates
are lower. However, most family reunions occur between May
and August. Former President Reagan proclaimed the first
weekend in August as Family Reunion Weekend[4].

Some families, like the Barcus family of Illinois annually
hold their gathering at the same location on either the second or
third weekend in August. They have held their reunions with
the same format, location and basic date for so long they do not
mail announcements, although the date is stipulated in their
annual newsletter.

Length of time

"Toting sack lunches," one family wrote, "we annually
visit our family plot at the cemetery on Halloween." This was
the most unusual family reunion reported.

Many families prefer to meet on Sunday afternoon with
the event catered in a controlled atmosphere (community hall or

---

[4] UPI Las Vegas Sun, August 3, 1986

restaurant). Families with few young children preferred a no-host dinner and tour of night spots. Throughout the nation the most popular format is potluck picnics held at a local public park.

"A week," according to many contributors, "is just right, it allows time to become acquainted with family while being short enough to wish you had more time." The Wetheringtons of Colorado enjoy meeting during the off season at a local ski resort. A San Francisco family holds their annual reunions aboard a cruise ship enroute to their native land. Those in the homeland prepare their homes to house the arriving guests.

Three-day weekends can be ideal as it allows enough time for a variety of activities. Start with a no-host dinner at a fashionable but moderately priced restaurant on Friday evening; a full day of activities on Saturday; Sunday could consist of tours. The diversified activities help stimulate communication between family members, and one activity is sure to appeal to some, some of the time. The three-day length justifies traveling expenses for families coming from afar.

Another popular form for reunions throughout Canada and the United States is camping. There are many reasonably priced attractive parks for self-contained recreational vehicles where children can expend energy in the playground, while adults discuss their heritage and exchange family recipes.

There are many combinations and considerations to budget procedures for clan gatherings. Usually, family units pay for the activities a member of their group participates in; however, a wonderful alternative is to have a single fee cover all expenses. This format encourages people to participate in more activities. Computing the amount to charge can be challenging

but definitely not impossible. The Trammell family of Texas
have the grandparents pay for their children and their respective
families. Whereas the Wetheringtons enjoy an all expense paid
reunion, including traveling expenses.

Harmony gives purpose and guidance to the event.
Genealogical research and achievement recognition are two
popular themes. Heritage motifs can be excellent as they offer
education for youngsters while seniors enjoy contributing
memories.

Displaying an easily read and understood family tree
can enrich the reunion experience for everyone as it gives an
overall view of the family. Two photographs in the artist
section reflect different styles. The Rauls of South Dakota use
an organizational chart, unfortunately a photograph was not
available.

PROGENITOR

1st GEN -   1st GEN.   1st GEN

2ND GEN   2ND GEN   2ND GEN

Descendent and ???

An admirable trait in some families is welcoming each
and everyone who has ever been associated with the family.
Various divorced members of the Smith Family of northern
California recently gathered at 'grandma's', and each one was
lovingly welcomed! According to a news program, a wealthy
gentleman united all his extended and step-relatives by flying
everyone to his estate for the holidays. It sounds heroic; but
the fact is few families can achieve this utopia. Consider the
reaction of your family if Frank's 'ex'; Jane, attends with fourth
husband, while her second husband comes with his third wife.

In many families it is the more the merrier, but when abuse has been prevalent it may not be wise. Sometimes mere association or thought of a former traumatic experience is difficult to handle. On the other hand many 'ex's are closer to the family than the blood bond, but don't pick and choose who can attend. The executive board should determine the format. Many families include widows and widowers, as they have often invested a great deal of time with the family. Often these individuals have spent most of their adult lives participating in the family's activities, and not to include them would be cruel. Discussions may arise when a widow or widower remarrys then you will have to decide for your family.

Youngsters reared by a step-parent usually establish family bonds. However, when adults become step-children those ties are usually not as developed. Set a time when these step-children, adults, other family members can come, during desserts, games and the family program.

Adopted children should be treated as full descendants with the adoption notation being in the family record book. Usually, people outside the immediate adopting family need not know, unless the adoption is obvious, such as an adoption of older or different nationality children. Three India siblings, eight through fourteen, were adopted into our family last year. The clan is sincerely interested, and many members have actively extended a warm welcome.

In heritage may lurk kings and queens but more likely you'll discover a dandy of a skeleton or two. These scoundrels can slip through the labyrinth of confusion into oblivion, or be expounded upon and presented as a play. Living scoundrels and trouble makers, on the other hand, can pose a problem. Ann Landers addressed the situation on April 13, 1988, by stating when a 'black sheep' is trying to rehabilitate, he should be included. When people state they will not attend if so-and-so does, she recommends a, "Sorry, we will miss you" statement. The best policy is to invite everyone, for to exclude anyone can cause permanent 'uniting' damage to the over-all event's acceptance. Reunions can increase self-esteem which is so often desperately needed by the less fortunate. For chronic behavior and anti-social personalties, check with your local mental health department for their recommendations on how to handle your particular situation. Sometimes the situation can be handled discreetly and efficiently without anyone's knowledge of your watchful eye.

As the president or general coordinator you will want an overall picture of the responsibilities and activities of each officer, department or committee.

It really is a rewarding activity.

FAMILY REUNIONS AND CLAN GATHERINGS

Vice President or Site Coordinator

Locate and prepare sites for the event. Be sure the sites selected are neither too large, elaborate, or too small and modest to fit your families needs. Some families prefer controlled to out-side environments for their activities. Evaluate your family's interest what seems to be the predominate common denominator, other than being a descendent of the same progenitor? Golf? Tennis? Bowling? Boating? Fishing? Try to locate a site with lots of diverse activities available or within easy driving distance. Figure travel time between sites, if it will be a progressive event. Check accessibility and comfort for everyone at the various sites. When a site is not accessible for the handicapped, be sure to notify those members to compromise or solve the problem.

When few relatives know those beyond their immediate nucleus, a neutral site is better. Sites within an hour's drive of the family core typically assure longer participation especially by the younger adults. Areas too convenient to home encourage a drop-by-and-leave attitude, but does encourage family friends to visit. Don't you just love it when a person presents so many opposite viewpoints? Definitely gives you more angles to consider in selecting a site, though.

Outside events should have alternate plans for inclement weather. School gymnasiums, auditoriums, churches, conference rooms and resorts typically require advance reservations, oft times with a non-refundable deposit.

A family member's generous offer to hold the event on his ranch can be great or a disaster. Be sure to check the site for parking, restroom facilities, children's play area, and location for arranging tables, benches and other items. Throughout most of the nation, portable sanitation facilities can be rented.

Dude ranches can be excellent. Most of these accommodations include meals, lodging and activities on a per person flat fee. These facilities are usually quite comfortable and prepared to handle groups. If this is your choice inform them of projected attendance, when and other particulars as soon as possible. Make reservations early as some resorts have a two year waiting list.

Many park systems operate on a calendar year basis. As close to the first of the year as possible reserve your choice. Public parks often have rules which vary from park to park. For instance, some parks will not allow amplifiers; prohibit alcohol. Reservation park headquarters locations vary. For county parks, try the county courthouse; city parks, try city hall; some federal parks and national forests use MisTix 1-800-283-CAMP. Tickatron is a ticket agency for many locations and attractions their number, if applicable, should be in your local phone book. Private parks should be contacted directly. Another valuable source of information is your local chamber of commerce.

Group camping can be delightful or a miserable experience, With your goal to have a "Thank goodness I came" event ask questions; Is tent camping allowed? What is the maximum length for recreation vehicles? What does "full hook-ups" include? What is meant by 'improved grounds'? Are there laundry and shower facilities? Does the use fee include access to sport areas, equipment? Are there specific campground rules? Have the information available for anyone requesting it.

IMPORTANT:

Be sensitive to your handicapped and senior citizen's needs. Wheel chairs, crutches and other handicapped equipment usually functions better on concrete walk ways than on unimproved grounds. Restroom facilities should be near the main activity site.

Be sure the site committee has a plan for inclement weather. Many sites require a non-refundable deposit, so if the park systems has a gazebo or other means of protection reserve it FAST! Enthusiasm remains higher with diversified activities. Work with the activities coordinator to find a site with various options.

Secretary or Publicity Coordinator

Allow your warm personality to shine as you maintain the executive board minutes, compile and distribute news letters, and press releases.

Family newsletters should be friendly, enthusiastic, informative and instill the desire to participate by working with a committee, and sharing heirlooms. Determine a theme for the newsletter which reflects or is the same as the reunion's. Heritage, a popular theme, is one of the easiest and most fun. It allows for a great deal of creativity. Having an alligator, dressed for Florida fun, jump from a box could be appropriate for a Florida or Island gathering. Ah, don't fret, there are many drawings available for your use. Clip art books contain a collection of copyright free: sketches, caricatures, drafting of simple to complex drawings, sometimes even photographs. Dover Publications[5] accepts minimum orders and has a diverse supply.

The best formula for developing good newsletters is to review those you receive. What is it that you like or don't like about them? Keep a running list of the samples you prefer so

[5] Dover Publications, Inc. 31 East Second Street, Mineloa, N.Y. 11501

you can incorporate those techniques. Regardless of the format, keep the newsletters packed with enthusiasm, ask for suggestions, criticism and input. Try to word the newsletter to encourage "yes" responses. Stimulate your family to participate. Always include the date, reunion headquarters or office address, and phone number.

Advertisers know it usually takes three applications to achieve an impressive response. Typically, the first time people hear, read or see something new it is forgotten. The second contact usually registers with the subconscious. The third contact frequently makes one believe a friend recommended the item or event. The "three technique" is recommended for first time family gatherings. The first mailing could be an intention flyer mailed about a year before the anticipated event date. This early mailing gives families time to schedule their vacations during the event. The second mailing should contain specifics, price, location, and activities. Genealogical forms, a simple but accurate map of the reunion area, and brochures on local attractions are often included with this mailing. The third mailing depends upon the response from the previous mailings, can be used as a confirmation or last chance letter.

Type all the information going into the newsletter, and make sample layouts. There are many combinations and options. Some newsletters are printed on both sides of an eight-and-half-by-eleven inch or an eight-and-half-by-fourteen inch sheet of paper. The next step is an eleven-by-seventeen inch sheet of paper which can be folded to a typical eight-and-half-by -eleven inch format. Most writing should be at an eighth to tenth grade level. Column reading is easier to read than an eight-and-half inch wide page.

Headings should carry impact and arouse curiosity.

Print in bold type or use press-on letters. Press-on letters are available at many stationary houses. Up to three variations of lettering styles (fonts) and sizes can add interest and ease in readability. Try to select fonts that are complimentary.

Computers are definitely advantageous in developing newsletters. There are numerous options with fonts and size flexibility available in many computer software programs. Hand-written notes can add a friendly touch and call attention to a specific, if the basic newsletter is typed. Open spaces allow the eyes to rest or call attention to an important subject. When you have determined how much space your newsletter will utilize, decide which is the best method for mailing. If it is a single piece it can be folded to double as its own envelope. If other pieces will be included use an envelope which may be more expensive but is easier from a secretarial perspective.

When the information is ready for printing, proof and reproof the newsletter. Have the president proof the newsletter before mailing. Check the spelling of names. According to Shipley Associates[6] the basic symbols to use in proofreading and editing are:

ℓ Delete or take out.

∧ Insert a phrase, word, or punctuation mark.

∿ Transpose letters, words, or phrases.

⊐ Move to the right.

⊏ Move to the left.

≡ Use capital letter(s).

／ Use lower-case letter(s).

◡ Close up a space.

Add a space.

Make a new paragraph.

[6] Editing and Proofreading Symbols, STYLE GUIDE, Shipley Assoc. '90. p. 69-70

FAMILY REUNIONS AND CLAN GATHERINGS

The key is to be consistent with the symbols regardless of how many proofread the material. Each proofreader should use a different color so the writer will know the person suggesting the change.

Here's a practice sample:

writers and Sectaries o word pro cessing specalists have to agree on what to use when editingand proofreading drat materials.without, such an agreement, and a consistent convetion, erros kreep in and quality writing is impossible.

Edited with the aforementioned symbols:

writers and Sectaries o word processing specalists have to agree on what to use when editingand proofreading drat materials.without such an agreement, and a consistent convetion, erros kreep in and quality writing is impossible.

Agree on what symbols to use before editing and proofreading draft materials. Without an agreement errors creep in and quality writing is impossible. If you would like a complete set of proofreading symbols use The Chicago Manual of Style[7], or the United States Government Printing Office Style[8].

The main thing to remember is consistency. Decide upon a format and follow it throughout your writings, ie: Grayson plant not Grayson Plant with Edison high school, or Reunion Company to Family Co.

All this about proofreading reminds me of a letter a dear friend, Ev Morris wrote. "Writers are a breed apart from most other artists. Painters do not gather in small groups and throw oil paint or water color at each others' creations.

---

[7]The Chicago Manual of Style[7], 13th edition, p. 94,

[8]United States Government Printing Office Style Manual (March 1984) p. 5.

Sculptors rarely or probably never throw globs of clay, or rocks, at their fellow artists' creations. The fact is, writers deal in thoughts and ideas, and words are our media. As an integral part of our learning, we traditionally critique each others creations." So have your material proofread, it can save embarrassment. The proofreader should make suggestions without being vindictive or faultfinding.

Family newsletters are usually photocopied or printed at quick press shops. To keep photographs from copying as black blobs on photocopiers use a "copyscreen". It is a series of little white dots which causes the copier to see the black mass in individual spots, therefore retaining some of the clarity of the original photograph.

Spots of color increase the price. Each color is a separate run on the printing press. Some color photocopiers can print colors in a single run. These machines achieve fairly good results and are becoming more cost efficient, although for group runs may still be too expensive.

Sharpest clarity and consistent quality can only be achieved through a full print shop. Each color is applied individually, which increases the per piece cost. All color photographs require four color process, and a technical color separation. Gang (grouped together) printing photographs can reduce costs slightly in some instances, especially in book formats.

Postage fees are a major concern. By adding a single piece of paper the rate per letter can jump, almost double. There are some alternatives to consider; one is to design the mailer to function as its own envelope which reduces postage. Some families in an attempt to economize mail the newsletters to a specific generation with the assumption that the word Cont. pg 48

45

PRINTER'S JARGAN
TO HELP YOU IN THE PRINTING MAZE

Camera-ready copy - The printer takes a picture of your final copy to
make plates for the presses. When you have made all corrections
and printed a version on a laser printer or image setter, it is said to
be "camera- ready".

Color separations - To print more than one color you need more than
one negative - one for each color in the final print. Therefore, even
though you can see all the colors on your screen, when you print
camera-ready copy, you must print one copy for each of the four
colors of ink. See "full color printing".

Film - Printing film is used as the negative for plates. The printer
makes film on a stat camera or directly on an imagesetter. Most
service bureaus (companies with image setters, linotronic and other
high end printers) will ask if you want it on RC paper or film. Film
eliminates a step for the printers, therefore clarity is often sharper.

Full-color printing - Also called four-color printing or process, is
using a full palette by mixing: cyan (blue), magenta (red), yellow
and black inks. Spot color are usually specified ink color. Panatone
is the most popular and accepted color guide.

Halftone - Artwork with shades or gray or tones of color, especially a
photograph, will not reproduce using printing inks. The artwork is
therefore turned into patterns of dots to achieve the effect of tones.
When you look closely at photographs in a newspaper you can see
the dots. Higher resolution (smaller dots) can be used for finer
results. Most laser printers print at 300 dots per inch (dpi) while
imagesetters can go to 2540 dpi. Halftones and screens are usually
measured in lines per inch (lpi).

Imagesetter - Essentially a high-resolution printer. It uses a
photographic process and wet developer rather the dry toner

system of office laser printers. The result is a very sharp image suitable for high-quality printing and color separations.

Plain-paper printer - These are laser printers with resolutions of up to 1000 dpi, which is equivalent to the lower resolution of imagesetters.

Plates - Offset presses use plates to carry the image to paper. Plates are made by passing light through film to expose the photosensitive surface. Metal plates are higher quality and last longer, but paper plates are less expensive and can be produced directly in an imagesetter.

Resin-coated (RC) paper - Also called repro, for reproducible film.

Resolution - A measure of relative density of ink, toner, or dots on your screen.

Screen - Even though the ink is black (or one of the CYMB colors) you can get a gray background by specifying a percentage of black. The finer the shading of gray or color, the greater the number of lpi of screen you need. Screens are tricky and can easily cause problems if you don't check with your printer first.

Stat camera - Printers use stat cameras to photograph your camera-ready copy and create the film for plate making. Stat is short for electrostatic, but the process is now entirely photographic.

Stripping - Traditionally, halftones and typeset copy were supplied separately, and stripped together to make the final negative. Some people still find it more efficient to let the printer strip in the photographs for the desk top publishing (DTP) newsletters.

Typesetting - What you couldn't do before there was personal computers with DTP software. Typesetters were the people who had type libraries and actually put type on the page, or added it to your artwork before it went to the printer.

will reach everyone. I strongly urge you to send invitations to all households. Each family should be acknowledged and encouraged to participate leaving no doubt as to their welcome.

Zip codes are a means for the postal service to divide the country into geographic areas or cities. The first three numbers indicate an area or city, the last two identify the zone or post office. The Zip + Four programs adds four more identifying numbers. These numbers specify an area within a city, or identify a corporation, large building and route. Although the '+ Four' numbers identify the route it does not specify the carrier. Numbers were used in zip codes due to their ease in readability, and their capability to become bar codes which computers can be programmed to read. Thus, computers sort the mail to a large degree. The local postmaster added, "In the foreseeable future computers will be able to read the second line of an address as well. Therefore, it is necessary to use the three line address format."

The use of zip codes also allows many families to achieve lower postal fees through non-profit, bulk or periodical mailings. All have restrictions.

Second-class mail is for periodicals and offers good service if you can qualify for a permit. Your newsletter can be considered a periodical if five hundred or more copies are addressed and mailed quarterly. There is a one-time charge of $265 plus.

Non-profit and not-for-profit groups must meet certain criteria and comply with government regulations. This is discussed more in the treasurer/budget section.

Bulk rates on the other hand are available and usually profitable for group mailings of over eight hundred. They must be copies of a single printed material with nothing added or deleted. Apply for a bulk rate number at the post office where the pieces will be mailed. The bulk rate number is valid for a full calendar year. The bulk rate box goes on the envelope or envelope section in the upper right hand corner. If

```
BULK RATE
U. S. Postage
   PAID
Permit No. 62
Yreka, CA 96097
```

it will be part of the folded newsletter you can print this box as the newsletter portion is being printed, if there is already printed material on the back page there will be no additional printing charge. Be sure to notify the treasurer of the bulk rate permit fee, and anticipated mailing expenses.

Bundle matching zip codes together. It takes a minimum of ten pieces to receive a discount in that specific zip code area. Before postal rate increases pieces could be mailed for nine cents, some businesses received even lower rates. Software database programs can print addresses according to the zip code which simplifies the sorting process. The person in charge of coordinating your family's addresses may have a computer and a software program with this capability. There are many programs available some with merging capabilities so that each piece could be personalized.

The *boxed* sample newsletters contain text only, so be sure to be creative in your motivation techniques. The Gundlach-Poirot Family of Illinois have shared their 'invitation and announcement' newsletter samples. They added that much of their knowledge came from an article Dorothy Ansburgey Griffith wrote on Family Reunions.

The first newsletter should be mailed close to a year before the scheduled event, especially for first time gatherings. Dynamic, enthusiastic, and proud, are adjectives for this initial mailing. You must stimulate enough motivation to make the

Sample of newsletter covers* from across the nation.

* Hilborn's Family Newsletter Directory cover. I have tried to reach this company but without success...apparently the company no longer exists.

Family reunions are an excellent opportunity to: perpetuate the memory of ancestors; gather genealogical information; share family stories, history and anecdotes; get reacquainted; meet relatives and over-all have a good time.

LETS HAVE ONE!

When - approximate month

Where - general vicinity

What - describe possible itinerary (dinner Friday night, barbecue; Saturday main event - list some activities, historic tour Sunday).

Expenses- (indicate a nominal fee will be charged but exact amount not yet determined.)

It is impossible to estimate attendance, but are you interested?

Help us plan now!

Send the names and addresses of other descendants. Discuss this with your family members and help spread the word. Next summer you will receive an announcement letter with more details. In the meantime, please advise the committee how many plan to attend in your group.

All information, suggestions, comments, questions are welcomed and encouraged.

We need your help.

Committee , date and address

This allows families to schedule vacations and make other necessary travel arrangements. Communities develop a specific theme; mining in the gold country, theater in New York, Shakespeare and white water in Oregon, to snorkeling in Hawaii. By listing the areas' points of interest visiting family members can plan their free time activities; and bring appropriate clothing. Recommend casual or formal attire for questionable activities. If the budget can afford it send local brochures as this will encourage people to come.

SMITH CLAN GATHERING!

When (dates)

Where (location)

The festivities will begin (date) with warm welcomes. Unveiling of the current (surname) family tree. Be sure to complete and return your family history to ensure proper information is recorded on the family tree. (Describe the main site attractively to stimulate attendance.)

.... is the host/hostess. He has made arrangements with various families to house or meet you at the airport. He also has a list of motels and campgrounds in the local area where many of our groups will stay. If you have special concerns call or write (host/hostess).

Bring something to display and share. Donovan is bringing the crib Mary used in 1848 as she crossed the plains with her parents. Florence is bringing the vase her mother painted. Carl is bringing his grandfather's Model A Ford. Maggie is bringing an old photo album, she would like help identifying various photos. If you need something or some place special to display your treasured heirloom call (security). If you have old reunion movies or other items you think would interest the family bring them!

Let's have a heritage dance. Dancers and musicians, and seamstresses step forward! This can be a major event for our reunion.

The average (month) climate in (area) is (describe the temperature, rain, humidity and other pertinent factors). Note the local points of interest and state if a particular one will be a family group activity.

(For the Saturday picnic would: families within a 50 mile radius bring salads or a hot dish; within a 100 mile radius bring desserts; and globe trotters please pick up condiments, chips, olives, pickles and other goodies. The barbecue will start at 12:30. At 3:00 P.M. friends will join the group for dessert and fellowship. State if group reservations and additional fees for participation are required, be sure to note here.

All information, suggestions and questions are encouraged. Please volunteer...we need your help and expertise. List committees and respective chairpersons with phone numbers. Announce committees still needing chairpersons.

Date, sign with address.

All correspondence should be sent to the reunion address where it will be directed to the necessary committees.

---

family units want to attend a gathering, to meet family, to visit with cousins, and other extended family members. They need to see the benefits such a gathering might have for their children. Good times, fun, and fellowship...not to mention heritage, and family pride can be used as motivation tools.

The second announcement should be mailed four to six months before the occasion, packed with enthusiasm and energetic optimism. Recognize committee chairpersons (the magic of seeing one's name in print does wonders to stimulate more involvement). By the mailing of this newsletter include cost per various activities, or per person charge for all inclusive participation. The treasurer probably has the projected per person costs computed. Urge prepayment as this indicates a sincere intent to attend and protects the reunion funds.

Weather is always a major concern. The newsletter should include typical weather temperatures for the season with recommendations for sweaters or ski parkas. Humidity and chill factors should be mentioned if

Smith Clan Gathering

The reunion is rapidly approaching (dates). Be sure the committee has your family information and reservations confirmed for the additional activities. Don't miss this great occasion. (Estimate attendance. Let everyone know this is really going to be successful, a real "Thank goodness I came" event.)

Hurry time is running out.

Families needing accommodations or transportation please contact (name) at (phone number). Itemize activities with location, access and other directions relating to festivities. Draw a simple map and include it. (For the Saturday picnic would: families within a 50 mile radius bring salads or a hot dish; within a 100 mile radius bring desserts; and globe trotters please pick up condiments, chips, olives, pickles and other goodies. The barbecue will start at 12:30. At 3:00 P.M. friends will join the group for dessert and fellowship.

Discover your heritage.

Family reunion committee and address.

Thank all families

who have returned the registration and genealogical forms.

appropriate.

Registration, genealogical forms and a simple but accurate map of the areas included in the reunion activities should be drawn and sent at this time.

The third mailing, sent about 45 days before the event, can double as confirmation receipts or 'hurry up and make your reservations!' Print the messages on different colors. Yellow for delighted you're coming, and blue for what's wrong? Stress the importance of pre-registration and the value of the extended family and heritage.

The yellow confirmation letter can act as the identification ticket to your group. Even when the park system states it is not necessary, suggest family units bring them. Of course, if the park has their own tickets use those.

After the event report results, acknowledge those who traveled the greatest distance, the eldest, the youngest, champion fisher, golfer, whatever to motivate pride of attendance. This helps acquaint families and encourages attendance of future events. Thank the committee chairpeople (whose support will be needed for the next event). For annual or semi-annual newsletters, reiterate the importance of having news articles to the secretary six weeks before anticipated publishing date. Include an address list of all descendent families. (The Address Coordinator probably has this portion of the newsletter ready for use.) Either list addresses as on an envelope or alphabetically using the first name of the direct family member. This makes locating family members easier, considering the divorce rate currently prevalent in our country.

Smith Clan Gathering Event of the Decade

(or whatever) is over, but we've just begun!

We've just begun weaving family awareness, expanding horizons, and experiencing the joys of knowing one another. Discovering each other's noblesse, learning their interests, skills, and retelling of our 'family history'. Thank you each and everyone for making our first event so successful.

(month) and (year) will be our next reunion. For those who missed this opportunity don't take a chance on missing our second...mark your calendars now.

Summarize the highlights. (Approximately 300 people met at Emigrant Lake for the main day of the reunion. Hilda, 92, was the eldest and Drew, one week old, the youngest to attend the festivities. Drew is the son of Kathy and Gary. Traveling the farthest was Susan and family. All twenty boarded the plane in Tenbucktoo, grandparents through two month old, Karly.) Describe some of the heirlooms shared. (Barbara's husband, Joe, made a beautiful case to hold their family treasurers including an original Theodore Roosevelt Teddy Bear. Chuck is drawing a picture book of memories from the 'Old Place'...definitely a treasure!)

List the new officers including the president's address and phone number. Publicize the photo collection, prints of the family tree and other items. Request information for the next newsletter to arrive at least a month before scheduled mailing. List the branch reporters or coordinators.

Thank the committee chairpersons, workers and attendees.

Address and Date

News Releases

Journalism is tight, factual writing whereas newsletters are friendly and informative. The leading sentence should summarize the article in a manner that will intrigue the reader and encourage him to read the article. A typical lead-in could tell a few of the pioneer families early contributions to the local area summing up with "descendants will gather for a family reunion." Another popular lead-in is the use of a famous family member; national senator, movie star, or Pulitzer prize winner.

Many local newspapers prefer articles with photographs. Black and white photographs are preferred but with modern technology many newspaper offices can use colored prints. Black and white film often takes two weeks to develop; however, some society page editors can issue a roll of the newspaper's film which they are prepared to develop in most instances.

People are often disappointed when their articles are edited, re-written, and otherwise revised. By working with the editor and writing in accordance to their guidelines gives one a better chance of being published. Although nothing will assure that your article will be published, let alone as you submitted it. Some local news papers print announcement press releases, but more often is the post article. Remember, keep the article factual, interesting and submit within two weeks of the event.

A standard format is to type when possible, otherwise print very plainly. Editors seldom read hand-written material. Use active verbs, be factual and informative. Use only white eight-and-half-by-eleven inch paper. Be sure that there are ample margins (minimum three-fourths of an inch) on all sides. Single space in the upper left hand corner your name, address and phone number. In the upper right hand corner put "News Release." IMMEDIATE RELEASE in capital letters, if applicable, release date, and black and white (B/W) photograph. (The photograph should have your name, and phone number on the back. Write lightly to not damage the picture.) Make a line across the page then double space the article. Keep the information to a single page, absolutely no more than two pages. At the end of the article center "###."

Write, edit, re write - edit, then have the president or executive board edit. Double check the spelling of names.

FAMILY LIFE

Shari Fiock
P.O. Box 1854
Yreka, CA 96097
Phone: 916 842-5788

News Release
IMMEDIATE RELEASE
January 1, 1990
B/W photo (please return)

Organizing group events, including family reunions and clan gatherings, are challenging at best, but with the newly released how-to book, "Family Reunions and Clan Gatherings" it becomes easier. Shari Fiock of Yreka, California has traveled throughout the United States meeting family reunion and clan gathering organizers for the past six years. Most family reunion organizers believe 'family' is the nucleus of civilization. They were eager to share their experiences to help you develop "Thank goodness I came" and not "Why'd I bother" events. They have found the benefits of uniting extended family beneficial and would like other families to partake in reviving this lost tradition. In addition to the anecdotes of various families throughout the Nation, the book includes a time frame calendar, constitution, delegation guidelines, and other helpful recommendations.

Fiock, noted in Marquis' Who's Who of American Women, has operated a public relations firm for many years, and is currently the West Coast Representative for the National Writers Club. Fiock says, "In our mobile, stress-filled lives, too often the importance and benefits of the extended family are forgotten. To perpetuate the foundation of a life long loving support network group, organize your clan gathering now."

Books are available at the BOOKSTORE, or by writing Coyote Publishing, P.O. Box 1854, Yreka, CA 96097.

###

127 designs each in two sizes

91 cuts

180 cuts!

Clip art samples from Dover. Leave a narrow cut border around the cut, use white-out if necessary.

Treasurer

Anyone appointed with this job is familiar with bookkeeping procedures; therefore, on to family reunion or clan gathering budgets. Most families found establishing a saving or money market account then switching to a checking account as the event approaches advisable. This is fine as long as there is enough money to earn interest; however, in many instances when the balance is too low, bank charges can dwindle funds. For savings accounts which are not earning interest, put the money in a safe deposit box between reunions.

Be sure to note the final date to obtain group tickets, reimbursement for unused prepaid activities, and refunds. If reserved tickets are not returned or cancelled before that specific attraction's cutoff date, full payment is due. Many families use envelopes to hold the tickets, with the purchasing family's name and activities paid for in advance noted on the front. Once the family picks up the envelope it is their responsibility. Some families had sign-off sheets stating that the tickets had been picked up by the specified family.

The supply coordinator has probably checked the

store's policy to assure that refunds of unopened plastic or paper products can be returned for a full refund or credit.

Other considerations are discussed in the formation of the executive board. Be prepared to respond if you are asked about the virtues of obtaining a non-profit, or not-for-profit status. Should your family want more information on this issue, contact an attorney (preferably a family member) for advice. There are some benefits, especially if the organization plans to offer family scholarships, have a revolving loan fund, or similar concerns that may outweigh the headaches of inviting bureaucracy red tape.

Working with the executive board, try to project attendance so that the overall cost may be divided amongst the attendees.

- ❑ Long distance telephone calls.
- ❑ Film and developing.
- ❑ Name tags.
- ❑ Material for signage.
- ❑ Emergency fund.
- ❑ Trophies for the activities committee.
- ❑ Printing.
- ❑ Stamps, postage and postage fees.
- ❑ Address labels or envelopes.
- ❑ Professional services.
- ❑ Decorations.

Food and beverage budgets need to be accurately compiled;

- ❑ Food.
- ❑ Table covers.
- ❑ Napkins.
- ❑ Paper plates.
- ❑ Paper, plastic or ceramic cups.
- ❑ Plastic utensils.

Deposits may be required on:
- ❑ Carbonated beverages.
- ❑ Kegs.
- ❑ Site reservations.
- ❑ Sports equipment.

Genealogy and Family History budgets can vary extensively.
- ❑ Research books.
- ❑ Forms.
- ❑ Possibly computer software.

One family received a start-up fund of almost $400.00. They erroneously projected this would secure site fees, cover intention newsletter mailing with a cushion to start the event as the gathering took place in the family's hometown with a pot-luck menu. The money collected as attendees prepaid, $3.00 per person with children six and under free, would cover: hamburger and buns, paper and plastic products, and beverages. The committee believed lots of items could be borrowed but there was just not enough. A single sheet of paper doubled the per envelope mailing costs, a keg of beer, carbonated beverages, and numerous long distance phone calls spelled doom to the budget. A donation box remained empty. When some family members learned of the financial plight, they contributed generously.

In other words, be careful. Hidden costs or advance group reservations without reimbursement can definitely dampen a gathering's "Thank goodness I came" goal.

FAMILY REUNIONS AND CLAN GATHERINGS

Activities

Diversified activities, competition, ice breaking games and other exercises to stimulate communication will help make the event a "Thank goodness I came" and not a "Why'd I bother?" memory. A dear deceased friend from Holland, a self imposed family black sheep, stated their reunions were "heart wrenching disappointments of constant competition and social climbing achievements." How sad he felt that way, but we can remember his evaluation and plan events to offer something special for everyone.

First, with the president and executive board, decide upon a theme for the entire event. A general theme gives each officer and worker a framework or foundation upon which to build for a common goal. Once a theme has been decided, of course, you should apply it to the activities. For instance, if heritage was the primary goal, have performances in period costumes, singing songs of the appropriate time, and dances or dance troops performing during the program. Having a skit of an ancestor's exceptional experience, or even portraying their daily life style can be rewarding especially when youngsters are

63

motivated to act out the incident.

Shyness is puzzling, even close friends can become withdrawn amongst a group of strangers - yes even family. This can spell disaster to the overall success of the event; therefore, plan activities from the very onset to offset this dilemma. One excellent way is the use of a large graphic family tree (techniques to create are in the signage section). This method offers everyone an opportunity to see how they fit into the extended family picture along with the stranger standing beside them. Some people are stunned to learn whom their extended family includes.

If your family is a 'game playing' family, here are two excellent versions of Bingo. As each family member completes registration, give him a sheet of lined paper and pencil. The object is to gather as many signatures of attendees as possible with all right handed people signing with their left hand (and visa versa). The person who collects the most signatures wins. Beware, a duplicate signature cancels the entire entry and that collector cannot play. Another version on the same theme is to give each member a sheet of paper divided into squares (twelve minimum, a hundred maximum). Each player's name should be written on a separate piece of paper, folded and put into a container upon registering. The player circulates among the family collecting a different signature in each square. During the program complete the game. Issue enough un-cooked beans to cover each square. Draw a name from the container and have the players place a bean in that square. Continue drawing names until someone has a row (vertical, horizontal, or diagonal) covered. These activities encourage circulation. As each person's name is called ask him to stand, this increases familiarity.

FAMILY LIFE

A few families used sharing of first experiences to break the ice. The "first" can be a picture of a grandchild, trip abroad, adventure. As the extended family becomes better acquainted, incorporate aspiring actors and actresses to dress and don the personality of deceased family members, then perform skits recapturing historic family moments. Recently I attended a performance at the Black Swan, part of the Shakespearean theater in Ashland, Oregon. The skit opened a few days before Christmas as five family members gathered for the holidays. They opened a treasured box of Christmas tree ornaments. Remembrances began. By adding a sweater or removing a scarf, these five people transcended eight generations to the time the ornaments were given to a married daughter. The daughter left the old country and sailed on the Mayflower. The ornaments then passed to another and the skit continued through the years. This was a professional performance, but the theme could be applied to many families, especially those with aspiring playwrights, actors, and actresses. The seniors will love to be involved in remembering dear ones, their antics, unique walk, speech and other traits to breathe life into the character. Work closely with the master of ceremonies, program coordinator as some of these recommendations overlap. Besides, it is imperative to keep unity throughout the event.

Viewing of family heirlooms from jewelry, photo albums, Model A Fords and other mementos, is a wonderful stimulant. Most families found this to be a natural step in uniting; however, a few families said this caused trouble when someone felt the current owner had obtained the piece inappropriately. Some families set a special area aside for viewing. This is discussed more fully in the security section.

From an ice-breaking beginning, build to a memorable

crescendo. One of the most popular formulas is to have a few ice breaking activities with visiting the primary function before the meal. Enjoy the meal, then an hour-or-so program, and followed with more fellowship. This format is known as the 'hour glass'. (For business applications, start with a subject of mutual interest or concern, possibly a keynote speaker, followed by a workshop.) Each day should have a climax, but the main event must build to a memorable crescendo. An easy one is to use helium balloons attached to an eighteen inch colored string. Hand out the balloons and have everyone join hands. Perform a follow the leader dance through the area. Parade through the heirloom area, past the eldest and youngest family members, coat-of-arms, Bible or special features such as the graphic tree, a beautifully decorated cake, etc. Wind into a spiral then at a specified moment or sound, release all the balloons in unison.

An alternate to this format is with the issuance of the balloon, include a piece of paper and writing instrument. Ask them to write a message they would like to hear. Tie it onto the balloon's string. Have them look about and spot someone they have not had the opportunity to meet or speak to at this gathering. Ask them to exchange balloons, etal with that person. Then as the exchange is complete have everyone release the balloons in unison. Still another popular option is to insert your name and address inside the balloon with a message asking the individual who finds it to please notify you. This option can have very interesting results. Sometimes the wind currents can carry these balloons great distances.

Recently I heard an environmentalist expound upon the dangers of releasing helium balloons outdoors. His theory was, ocean fish might eat the colored deflated balloons and make them sick, and metallic balloons might cause electrical blackouts if they become entangled with power lines. This is mentioned for your consideration.

Work closely with the executive board and all committees in unity for the events overall success. Offer a variety of activities. For the primary grades and younger, sack and relay races, hide and seek, are good activities. Young children and many adults enjoy competitive sports. Perhaps a teenager would like to be the assistant activity director and coordinate activities for young children, or a specific age group.

The site committee will know if there is sports rental equipment available at the site. If not, compile a box with: baseball, soccer, volleyball and other sport equipment your family enjoys. Appoint someone to monitor (sports quartermaster) the box to assure that all equipment is returned. The sports quartermaster may be called upon to settle disputes. Therefore, before starting the games clarify the rules. Fishing, golfing and other adult activities can be adapted for competition if your family enjoys competitive action.

Creating a family cookbook, or making a quilt are two alternatives many women enjoyed.

Have a photograph collage of previous reunions near the large graphic tree (signage committee), or have photograph albums available. With camcorders lending themselves so well to the movie industry, you may want to have a family documentary running on a television. Of course, networking conversation is the ultimate goal, so have most activities as options rather than mandatory participation.

Campfire activities abound: roasting marshmallows, popping popcorn, sing-a-longs, and much more. Heritage songs, story telling and reminiscing are good campfire activities. Children often know a variety of animated songs such as

"Swing Low Sweet Chariot." When the chorus sings "swing low" everyone should use a deep, low voice, clasps hands to form a cradle, and sway to-and-fro. Change the voice to jostling during the "sweet chariot" portion. Continue reacting to the verse throughout the song. Your local library probably has books on songs, games, ice breakers, and similar activities.

In preparation for the event accumulate brochures, costs, and pertinent facts for attraction near the area. Diversify and include activities for everyone. Some prefer theater to equestrian outings, others' golf to boating, baseball to swimming, fellowship to competition. Most tourism or chamber of commerce offices have local brochures. Contact the sites that would make good group activities to see if they have group options. What are the sites' rates? When are they able to accommodate your group?

Determine with the executive board the best procedure to handle reservations. Some families preferred getting the group discounts by having all reservations made by this committee; whereas, other families preferred having each family responsible for their own reservations and payments. Experience has shown that group activities unite families quicker in addition to qualifying for group discount rates. However, if collecting for the tickets is difficult have each family unit organize their own elective options.

For historic tours retracing your ancestors, contact the current owners of the house, business, or land to see if it would be possible to include the site in a tour. Many current owners will welcome you and may like to participate during the time you're at his location. Do not over-stay your welcome at any location, nor let the family's enthusiasm wane. Experience will be a great guide, but if this is your first time half-an-hour per site is sufficient. That is, half-an-hour when everyone has gathered to hear or take part in the activity.

Draw a simple, but accurate map which goes easily from one site to another. Drive the tour noting driving time between sites, include the approximate arrival and departure times on the map that should be distributed to all caravan drivers before starting the tour.

Headstone imprints from the family cemetery can be excellent 'show and tell' souvenirs for children. To make a headstone imprint, use a large enough sheet of paper to cover the desired epigraph area. Many families use butcher paper, but it is rather stiff...some light weight papers work well. These are available at survey, blueprint or art supply stores. Team work results in better rubbings. One person should hold the paper still while the other does the actual rubbing with a soft leaded pencil, charcoal, or crayon. Make broad strokes back and forth on the paper over the desired area. After the design is 'lifted', spray fixative (available at most art supply stores) on the relief to secure it. This last step is mandatory to retain clarity of the image.

While on Tangier Island, Virginia, a small island in Chesapeake Bay, I saw this unusual epigraph: "Come all my friends as you pass by, behold this place where I lie, as you are now, so once was I. Remember you are born to die."

Donovan Rogers found this late 1800s epigraph on a ranch in northern California; "An arm of an angel put me here, but all the angels in heaven can't keep me here."

Write a brief synopsis for the announcement (second) newsletter that includes; cost, time, and duration of each suggested activity. Be certain the secretary has it in time to include with the second newsletter, with brochures of the local area , and the drawn map.

CHANGES OF OUR TIMES

Linda (Grein) Barcus gives a perspective of the changes many of you may be too young to consider:

"Born before 1940 we were before television, before penicillin, before polio shots, frozen foods, Xeros, contact lenses, Frisbees and the pill.

We were before radar, credit cards, split atoms, laser beams and ballpoint pens; before pantyhose, dishwashers, clothes dryers, electric blankets, air conditioners, drip-dry clothes -- and before man walked on the moon.

We got married first and then lived together. How quaint can you be? In our time, closets were for clothes, not for 'coming out of'.

Bunnies were small rabbits and rabbits were not Volkswagens. Designer Jeans were scheming girls named Jean or Jeanne, and having a meaningful relationship meant getting along well with our cousins.

We thought fast food was what you ate during Lent, and Outer Space was the back of the local theater.

We were before house-husbands, gay rights, computer dating, dual careers and computer marriages. We were before day-care centers, group therapy and nursing homes. We never heard of FM radio, tape decks, electric typewriters, artificial hearts, word processors, Yogurt, and guys wearing earrings. For us, time-sharing meant togetherness — not computers and condominiums; a 'chip' meant a piece of wood; hardware was hardware, and software wasn't even a word!

FAMILY LIFE

In 1940 'Made in Japan' meant junk and the term 'making out' referred to how you did on an exam. Pizzas, McDonalds and instant coffee were unheard of.

We hit the scene when there were '5 and 10 Cent' stores where you bought things for five and ten cents. Sanders or Wilsons sold ice cream cones for a nickel and a dime. For one nickel you could ride a street car, make a phone call, buy a Pepsi or enough stamps to mail one letter and two postcards. You could buy a new Chevy Coupe for $600, but who could afford one? A pity, too, because gas was only eleven cents a gallon.

In our day, cigarette smoking was fashionable, 'grass' was mowed, 'coke' was a cold drink, and 'pot' was something you cooked in. 'Folk music' was a Grandma's lullaby and AIDS were helpers in the principal's office.

We were certainly not before the difference between sexes was discovered, but we were surely before sex changes, we made do with what we had! And we were the last generation that was so dumb as to think you needed a husband to have a baby!

No wonder we are so confused and there is such a generation gap today."

This is one of the more challenging,
but definitely rewarding committees.
Please share your experiences
with future clan organizers by writing me.

FAMILY REUNIONS AND CLAN GATHERINGS

Addresses

Many addresses will be presented at the first organization meeting. As the preliminary tree develops names of living but missing relatives, may emerge due to the family sleuth's skills. Ask the older family members if they have the missing addresses. Next, check with the family genealogist, county or state historical societies, genealogical organizations, chamber of commerce office, and telephone books. Many libraries and most telephone companies have extensive telephone directory collections. If your family roots extend to foreign shores, some families found that country's midnight or grave-yard operators friendly and eager to help those of you searching for an unusual surname. When you find a relative, call or write. If you opt to call the foreign country be sure someone is available to translate.

Develop an address list for distribution to family and organizers. Address lists can be prepared as for envelope printing, or sorted by zip code, first or last names. Pre-glued labels are available. Mailing labels will be used by the secretary for distribution of the newsletters. The first mailing should take place a few weeks after the initial meeting, with the second about four months before the event, and possibly a third a month before. An address list should be distributed to families at the reunion, or with the fourth mailing.

Beverages

Be sure to have plenty of liquids available, preferably cold-cold or hot-hot. Some catering companies include beverages, but limit the quantity. Look in your local yellow pages for a beverage company. Many times they will deliver, set-up and pick-up the tanks and kegs. Sometimes they even include cups and ice. Hard liquor...I've never heard of a public park where this is permissible, but there is always a first time.

Smaller ice chunks chill dishes, and drinks better; however, it melts faster than ice blocks. Of course, if the event is to be held inside there is not the problem with keeping the beverages near their intended temperature.

For potlucks ask the supply committee if there are large coffee pots, and ice chests available. Many public parks have electrical outlets; however, if your group plans to rough it you will have to use camp style coffee pots. An alternative to numerous ice chests is a plastic lined new garbage can or barrel filled with beverage cans or glass containers scattered amongst ice cubes. As children have a tendency to open a can and leave it after a few sips, a less expensive alternative is to use carbonated tanks and syrup with eight or six ounce paper cups. Even more economical is the use of flavor aid, kool aid, lemonade, milk, and water. There are numerous attractive and delightful punch recipes available, too. These can be dressed up with the simple addition of a center wreath of frozen flowers, fruit or other delectable. Dairy products need to be kept cool as they do not tolerate heat. Perhaps one ice chest could be designated as the dairy cooler. Hot beverages can include coffee, tea, spiced cider, or hot chocolate.

Public park systems often restrict or prohibit alcohol beverages. If it is acceptable, beer kegs are usually more reasonable than individual cans. Wine is now available in attractive boxes and should be kept chilled. Forget retrieving funds through an unattended donation box...it simply is not sufficient, at least as a rule.

Have prices and alternatives ready for the treasurer to figure for per person charges which will be listed in the second newsletter.

There are some group beverage recipes in the recipe section.

Food

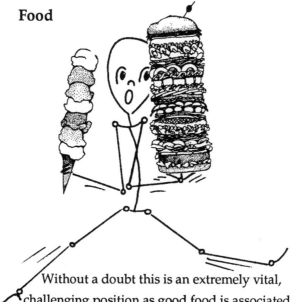

Without a doubt this is an extremely vital, challenging position as good food is associated with good times throughout the globe. Food, its preparation, quality, quantity and choice should reflect your family's preference: eastern or western European, Oriental, American, Native American, and vegetarian. Families emphasizing sports will have a different menu than the more sedate families. Quite often the all American hamburger wins the traditional family reunion barbecue debate. Except when the choice includes barbecued spareribs, and chicken. These options will be discussed further in this chapter. Evaluate your family to determine what format best suits the majority, and if possible discuss the options at a board meeting definitely with the president.

Another major decision is how many meals will you be coordinating? Some families have a special event day where everyone gathers, whereas some, like the Hall family of northern California, have a couple of weeks. Monica states their reunions are held at the family ranch with three meals a day for a week or more. Monica states, "Everyone contributes what they have in true potluck fashion. Then all the women gather in the kitchen to prepare meals. It becomes a real fun time. New brides are issued a sincere and warm welcome as she makes the salad. Kids run into the kitchen where every mother there, is eager to respond. It really builds a family unit - no matter how big."

One strong recommendation for serving breakfast is it gets everyone out of bed and energized for the day's togetherness. Dining locations need not be elaborate; work shops, scoured barns, lofty shade trees or star sparkled heavens. It is the bonding, the togetherness, that counts but good food sure helps. Try to get a general attendance count for the various meals.

Sometime during the reunion or gathering try to have a meal in tribute to your heritage. Perhaps members of the family could come appropriately attired. This can become a valuable tradition. Seniors love the attention to detail, and thrive on remembrances of the good ol'days. Benefits to the younger children are unmeasurable. They learn first hand what it means to be an American with a heritage from the old country.

The Herrera family of eastern Oregon perpetuate the pride of their ethnic backgrounds. Many of the men hunt in the traditional manner passing the skills and techniques of the arrow and spiritual communications to their children. The women prepare many of the dishes as their ancestors did before white man came. Deb-E adds, "Sometimes I prefer the more sanitary methods of grinding. Yuk, when I tried to grind the acorns with the mortar the rocks and dirt chunks were prolific. Nor do I serve feet stomped wine. Guess I've gone and gotten soft." As I see their children dance about the campfire in their tanned buckskin ceremonial robes, listen to the drums rhythm or watch the youngest son (then six years old) capture the interest of a group of teenage Boy Scouts by telling an Indian legend, there can be no doubt as to pride and confidence they possess. The Herrera's are a multi-national family, thus at their gatherings pinatas, sombreros, hat dances and tacos, just as the America's hamburger, apple pie and blue jeans make their appearance, too.

Potlucks

A meal dedicated to favorite dishes can perpetuate a heritage. Great-grandmother's favorite apple pie, or Aunt Betty's baked beans can become traditional fare at potlucks. It is nice to identify the dishes' originator, title and preparer's name. There are a number of ways to do this. Tape the identification label directly onto the dish or use free standing 'tents' (three-by-three inch stiff paper folded in half with the information written on the front). Part of the

> *Blushing Apple Pie*
> **In memory of:**
> *Merle Inze Purington Pruett*
> **Prepared by:**
> *Shari L. Fiock*

charm of potlucks is experiencing new and traditional food. Share recipes.

Nominal cost, diversification, and participation by all attendees makes potlucks a favorite. Some prefer surprise potlucks. (Once during a Boy Scout activity everyone made baked beans or potato salad! It was a great opportunity to analyze these two dishes - and a truly memorable potluck.) If this sounds too risky you might ask everyone whose first name (as many of you will have the same surname) starts with a specific letter: (A-F) bring hot dishes, (G-M) salads, (N-R) desserts, (S-V) beverages, (W-Z) condiments.   The division must be adapted to fit your specific needs.   A similar formula is to use mileage as the division factor.   Families within a fifty mile radius could bring salads or a specialty dish, those between fifty to a hundred miles might bring desserts.   Those coming the farthest could pick-up condiments at local convenience stores.

An attractive way to serve salads and other dishes that should be kept cool is with a "salad bar."   Use six-by-one inch, no smaller than two-by-four inch boards, and make a <u>deep</u> frame. A sturdy table can be its base with a heavy gauge plastic sheet forming the 'bowl'. Allow at least a six inch 'ruffle' to hang over the edge of the frame. Fill the cavity with ice chips so dishes can be nestled into the coolness. This will keep most perishable dishes safe during the meal, unless the table is in direct sunlight which can cause mayonnaise and many dairy products to spoil, jello to melt, and in brief render havoc.

Cater

The word 'cater' means to serve or provide food, and that is our next subject. Caterers are frequently independent service contractors who attain a reputation of exceptional food or service. Most companies prefer to work with you in develop-ing a meal that will appeal to your family.   A typical choice is a few meats, ie: chicken or roast; possibly eight salads including jello and vegetable; a starch like rice, potatoes or pasta; with beverage and dessert options.   It is advisable to have a fish dish on Fridays, and to order a percentage more for late comers. Prior to signing on the dotted line:

❑ Does the price include the site where the food is to be
    served or is this additional?

❑ Will the food be served buffet style or by dish to the
    individual?

❑ Can dishes prepared by individual family members be added?

❑ Does it include clean-up?

❑ What is the minimal deposit, and what is the latest date in case cancellation becomes necessary.

For 'formal' events figure ten servers with three kitchen helpers per one hundred guests.

Restaurants

Countless restaurants offer unique atmosphere, quality food and service. To help you determine which is the right restaurant for your group, first eliminate all the sites which cannot accommodate your estimated attendance. In many instances that will leave two or three options. Geographical location, size and capabilities of the chosen restaurant will all be factors in the monetary stipulations.

If your group is fairly small, fifty or less, the restaurant will probably honor a no-host option. This means that each person can order from the menu and receive a bill for that selection, but have the advantage of a group setting. For groups up to a hundred this option might be available if most guests will order a recommended item.   This item can be made even more attractive with a 'bargain' price. Once the group exceeds a hundred the restaurant will probably suggest a limited menu or buffet. Both are good choices even for smaller groups, especially if you do not want a lengthy interruption while orders are gathered.

The limited menu usually features two or three main dishes or meats with vegetables that compliment the chosen entree. This can be served as a buffet or delivered by the waitress or waiter to each individual.   Buffet option means an individual passes the food and selects items and quantity desired. (When serving this method at home or with others who are sharing their labors it is known as potluck. When each dish selected is charged separately it is commonly known as a cafeteria.) A typical buffet menu is:

Prime Rib of Beef

Deep Fried Prawns

Chicken Cordon Bleu

Twelve varieties of Salads

Cheesecake with Fresh Fruit

Chocolate Bavarian Pie

Coffee, Tea, Milk, or Sparkling Cider

This menu might cost anywhere from $18.00 to $40.00 per plate depending upon location and nominal charge of the restaurant.

Conference and convention rooms located within hotels, restaurants, and tourist attractions, may be quite noisy at various times of the day. Therefore visit the room during the time of day you expect your festivities to take place, especially if your group will be more interested in visiting than dancing.

The term, "wet bar" usually refers to alcohol, if your family will be doing quite a bit of drinking investigate the options. In many states there are laws which prohibit serving alcohol in the presence of minors . Although it is becoming less of a choice throughout the United States, some convention sites allow non-employees to prepare drinks in group situations. For hard (whiskey, bourbon, vodka, gin), and mixed (old fashions, martinis, manhattans, screw-drivers, etc.) drinks a qualified bartender is recommended. With such groups as MADD, SADD, and AA many sites no longer have hard liquor options. Beer and wine, although alcohol, are not as restricted. Be sure not to let anyone drive who has had too much to drink.

Predominately senior families on fixed incomes prefer sites that give senior citizen discounts.

Check with the coordinator to determine who is making the food and related activities selection. To enhance the event's success work closely with the president, site, and activity committees. The activity and program committees will probably arrange the dining tables, but the food chairperson should recommend a serving route for buffet, cater, and potluck service.

Traffic flow is a major consideration. The three most popular formats reflect basic geometric shapes; triangle, circle, and rectangle. Always try to have a 'replenishing route' so food can be added as needed.

The triangle format encourages the most mingling of guests when entries and exits are in proximity. When there is a single opening it should be at least five feet wide to allow ease in exiting with loaded plates. (It is always advisable to have a separate exit door.) One option is to have: plates, bread, salads, vegetables, condiments, meat, desserts, beverages and silverware surround the guests that are in the center of the room. A similar format, but opposite, is to have; equipment, food, and beverages on a large circular table with guests walking around it's edges.

The rectangle layout is good for narrow rooms with openings on either end. This often accommodates more people quickly and is quite adaptable. Recently I attended a function where the servers were in the center with two rows of guests walking past the tables, and the servers dished from the center. It worked very well.

Checklist of probable borrowerable items within family:

FAMILY REUNIONS AND CLAN GATHERINGS

- ❑ Folding chairs and benches.
- ❑ Card, folding, picnic tables.
- ❑ Lanterns, large flashlights, battery operated flood lights.
- ❑ Thermal ice chests.
- ❑ Large beverage containers.
- ❑ Barbecues or similar cookers.
- ❑ Hot plates.
- ❑ Large coffee pot.
- ❑ Be sure the items borrowed work before needing them during the event.
- ❑ Determine group meals, and prepare accordingly.
- ❑ Organize kitchen crews, if a number of meals are scheduled.

Beverages, if not assigned to another need to be computed.

- ❑ Quantity.
- ❑ Quality.
- ❑ Contracts for delivery and clean-up of kegs, tanks, etc..
- ❑ Be sure to ask a few people to serve on the clean-up crew. In rare instances, family members will stay to clean up, but too often it seems everyone assumes someone else will do the "mundane work."

Such Delicious Work!!!

Quantity and Quality

GROUP
COOKBOOK

During six years of interviewing clan organizers I was impressed with their enthusiastic and generous personalities. A prime example occurred just prior to printing this book when one of the those thoughtful individuals stated,

"My family really enjoys ' - '.
and I look forward to learning other family favorite dishes. "

My only regret is that this suggestion came so late that everyone couldn't share their recipes. Nonetheless, here are a few group recipes. Some contributors are noted for their cuisine skills: Cleo Antoine is the former owner of a Cajun catering company; Linda (Grein) Barcus is compiling a family cookbook; Jan Cozzalio has shared an entire proven menu, and a quantity formula; Thelma Davis has twenty years experience cooking for a public school; Ross Singleton is an 'official' pit barbequer; Yvonne Steinbring is a 4-H advisor/home-economists with the University of California; Jim Walker, a master barbequer, explains how to make a barbecue then cook tantalizing steaks; Mary Zubricky, former restaurateur, is compiling a cookbook; many other contributors share their exceptional preparations in this small, but important group cookbook.

Linda (Grein) Barcus shares:

SCRATCH AS SCRATCH CAN

My mother never let me do much in the kitchen except things like making vegetable salad, or stirring the gravy so it wouldn't be lumpy. As a result, my cooking knowledge and ability was practically non-existent when I got married. But I did remember mother mentioning to her many friends that she'd made certain cakes, pies and such from scratch. So, my first priority after the honeymoon was to locate some scratch.

With mother's delicious cakes in mind, my first trip to the supermarket was to buy some scratch. I found the aisle that read "Baking Items" and spent a good fifteen minutes looking at everything from Mazola Oil to corn starch, sugar, flour and chocolate, but no signs of scratch could I see. I was sure it couldn't be with pickles and mayonnaise, or in the meat department.

I asked a clerk if they carried scratch. He looked at me rather oddly and finally said, "Oh, you'll have to go to the store at the corner of Colfax and Wadsworth."

When I got there, it turned out to be a feed store. I thought this rather odd, but I guess cakes are food, so I went in and said, "I'd like to buy some scratch."

When the clerk asked me Cont'd pg. 88

BEVERAGE AND DIP

TEA FOR THE GANG
Serves 30
Debbie Fiock serves this cold or hot and it is always a favorite.

1 gallon medium strength sun tea
1 large can of frozen orange concentrate
1 large can of frozen lemonade concentrate
1 can pineapple juice
4 1/2 cups sugar
1 teaspoon cloves or 4 whole
1 teaspoon cinnamon or 1 stick

VERSATILE PUNCH
Mary Zubricky developed this delicious festive drink and states, "By adding rainbow or fruit sherbet with the fruit juice it makes a fruity drink that is not too sweet."

In a punch bowl place a
1/2 gallon rainbow, pineapple or lime sherbet
Equal amounts of:
Raspberry or cranberry flavored fruit drink
Pineapple Juice
7-UP or Ginger ale
Over the sherbet.
Serve.

COLORFUL DIP
A friend challenged me to create a colorful - festive dip and this evolved as a favorite amongst friends and family.

1 container of IMO
Equal amount of mayonnaise
1 cup sweet pickle relish
1 package green onion dip
(Fritos brand is good)
1 small jar of maraschino cherries
1 can of shrimp pieces, drained and rinsed

Dilute to desired thickness with milk to retain color brilliancy of pickles and cherries.

how much I wanted, I suggested a pound or two. His reply was, "How many chickens do you have? It only comes in twenty pound bags."

I really didn't understand why he mentioned chickens, but I had heard my mother say that she'd made some chicken casserole from scratch, so I bought twenty pounds and hurried on home, delighted with my purchase.

My next problem was to find a recipe calling for scratch. I went through every single page of my lovely "Better Homes and Gardens Cookbook" given as a wedding present but didn't find even one recipe requiring scratch. Subsequently, I spent hours in the nearby library trying to end my search. No luck. There I was with twenty pounds of scratch and no recipe.

When I had opened the bag of scratch, I had some doubt that a beautiful fluffy moist cake could ever result from such hard looking ingredients, but then, I was sure that with the addition of liquids and the use of heat, the results would be successful. I had no need or desire to mention my problem to my husband as he had suggested very early in our marriage that he liked to cook, and would gladly take over that department. One day when I was raving about his chocolate pie, he proudly acknowledged that he had made it from scratch, so I was assured that it could be Con't pg. 92

BREADS

Big Batch Muffins
Yield: 60 muffins
*Yvonne Steinbring makes these and bakes as needed,
"even for one person."*

> 2 cups hot water
> 2 cups shredded wheat biscuits (about 4)
> 2 cups All-Bran cereal
> 1 cup shortening
> 4 eggs
> 1 quart buttermilk
> 2 cups sugar
> 2 cups uncooked oatmeal
> 5 cups flour
> 5 teaspoons soda

Pour hot water over shredded wheat and All-Bran cereal. Add remaining ingredients in order given. Do not over-stir.

Will store in refrigerator in covered bowl 6 - 8 weeks. When needed, fill greased muffin tins (or use paper liners) 2/3 full and bake 20 minutes at 400 degrees.

Variation: Put a whole, pitted date in each greased muffin tin before filling with batter.

Refrigerator Rolls
Linda (Grein) Barcus states, "This dough can be kept in the refrigerator a week to ten days. It can be made ahead of time before the last minute rush is on."

> 1 cup sugar
> 1 cup oleo or butter
> 1 1/2 teaspoon salt
> 2 eggs
> 6 cups bread flour or all purpose flour
> 2 packages dry yeast
> 1 cup luke warm water

2 tablespoon sugar
1 cup boiling water

In two-cup container, dissolve yeast, 2 tablespoons sugar in luke warm water. Let rise (if it does not foam up in cup, do not use).

In mixing bowl, measure sugar, butter and salt in bowl. Pour boiling water over mixture. Blend and let cool some.

Add beaten eggs. Pour yeast in and mix. Add flour, slowly beating in well. It takes about 6 - 6 1/2 cups to make soft dough. (This dough will appear very loose. It cannot be handled with hands in this first stage.)

Cover and place in refrigerator at least four hours, preferably overnight. Make sure this is a deep bowl, it will rise above lid.

Take from refrigerator, dump on a floured board and knead. Place ball in well-greased bowl, cover and let rise at room temperature about three hours.

Punch down, place on lightly floured board, knead. Shape as desired. Place in greased pans, let rise to double, approximately 45 minutes, depending on temperature of room.

Bake at 375 degrees until brown or done.

Note: After the first kneading, it can be kept in the refrigerator until ready to use. Just keep air tight. You may also shape them and place them in greased pan, cover and place in refrigerator. Take out and let rise about three hours before baking. This is a very workable dough.

SOUP

VEGETABLE SOUP
Serves 24

Mary Zubricky writes, "I love the smell of soup simmering on the stove. I developed this recipe one damp, chilly day when the idea of soup was especially appealing."

2 medium onions, diced
2 stalks, celery, sliced in 1/2" pieces
6 Tablespoons. salad oil

4 carrots, sliced thin
4 small zucchini, sliced
2 large turnips, diced
4 to 6 leaves chopped kale, stems removed
4 quarts water

6 chopped fresh Basil leaves
      or 1 1/2 teaspoon. dried Basil
2 quarts tomato juice
4 teaspoon. salt or to taste
1/4 cup cider vinegar
2 teaspoon. Caraway seed (optional)

Saute onions and celery in oil until soft, about 5 minutes. Add second group of ingredients, bring to full rolling boil. Reduce heat, add third group of ingredients and simmer until vegetables are tender, about 30 minutes.

done.

Now, as many of you know, being a new bride is pretty scary, especially when three meals a day are on one's mind all the time. During the first weeks I learned that our muffins, waffles, pancakes, pies, cakes and even lemon pudding he'd made from scratch. Well, if he'd made all those things from scratch, I was sure he'd bought a twenty pound bag of it, too. But I couldn't find where he stored it. I checked my own supply, which I kept hidden in my side of the bedroom closet behind all my clothes, but it was still full.

The mystery continued, but I was never one to give up or reveal my problem. The biggest jolt came one day when I hear a friend bragging to my husband that he'd built his house himself from scratch. In quick succession I heard via numerous acquaintances that they'd made dresses, Halloween costumes, even jackets from scratch, in addition to their numerous desserts and pastries.

At this point, I was almost ready to give up because all the world seemed to know everything about scratch except me. But pride kept me silent. If paper can be made from wood, and glue from horse's hooves, maybe wood or cloth could be made from scratch.

By now, the detective in me was getting weary, so I decided to try Cont'd pg. 114

SALADS AND VEGETABLES

HEART PATIENT MAYONNAISE
1 pint
Cleo Antoine writes, "You may use 2 tablespoons vinegar instead of lemon juice. Also one tablespoon grated onion adds flavor. A couple of drops of yellow food coloring makes it look more like the real thing."

3 egg whites	1 teaspoon dry mustard
1 teaspoon salt	2 tablespoon lemon juice
1 teaspoon sugar	1 cup pure corn oil

In blender combine egg whites and salt; blend well. Add sugar and dry mustard. Blend and add half of oil. Blend and add rest of corn oil and lemon juice. Blend until thick. Store in refrigerator.

FRUIT SALAD
Serves 100
Mary Simmons contributes this mega salad.

1 quart lemon gelatin
3 1/4 quarts of boiling water
3 cups lemon juice
1 1/2 teaspoon salt
3 quarts + 1/2 cup of cottage cheese
2 No 10 cans of drained fruit cocktail
(reserve juice)
1 quart strawberry gelatin

Dissolve lemon gelatin in hot water; stir in 1 cup of lemon juice and salt. Cool until slightly thickened.

Fold in cottage cheese. Turn into 2 - 12" X 20" X 2 1/2" pans.

Chill until firm.

Add water to fruit cocktail syrup to make 3 1/2 quarts liquid; heat. Add strawberry gelatin, stirring until dissolved. Stir in remaining lemon juice; cool until slightly thickened. Fold in fruit cocktail. Pour over cottage cheese layer; chill until firm.

Do-Ahead Salad/Dessert
Serves 16 - 20
Evelyn (Runnels) Fiock states this is a Phillips family favorite.

1 14 oz fruit cocktail, well drained
1 cup fruit cocktail syrup, plus water if necessary
1 3 oz package strawberry flavored gelatin
1 8 oz package cream cheese, room temperature
1/3 cup salad dressing - your preference
1 cup pecan halves
20 maraschino cherries, quartered (1/2 cup approx.)
2 cups miniature marshmallows
1 pint whipping cream, whipped

Drain fruit cocktail thoroughly; reserve syrup. Measure syrup and add water to make 1 cup. Bring liquid to boiling point. Add gelatin stirring until gelatin is thoroughly dissolved. Chill mixture until slightly thickened and syrupy.

Beat cream cheese until fluffy; add salad dressing, and gelatin. Beat until mixture is smooth and free of all lumps. Fold in pecan halves, drained fruit cocktail, cherries, marshmallows and whipped cream.

Peach Ginger Ale Salad Molds
Yield: 6 1/2 quarts mixture 1/2 portions serves 50
"Sooooo simple and everybody likes. I added a blob of whipped cream to pretty it up," Jan Cozzalio writes.

8 3 oz packages (1 1/2 pounds) orange flavored gelatin
1 1/2 teaspoons salt
2 3/4 quarts hot water
4 No. 2 1/2 cans (2 1/4 quarts) drained, canned, sliced
   peaches
1 1/2 quarts ginger ale

Dissolve the orange gelatin and salt in hot water. Chill until slightly thickened. Fold peaches and ginger ale into slightly thickened gelatin. Turn into individual molds or shallow pans.

Chill until firm.

Unmold or cut in squares. Serve on crisp lettuce with mayonnaise or whipped cream salad dressing.

TOBOULEH
Serves 40 - 50
"There are many versions of this Middle Eastern Salad. It is a delicious complement to almost any main dish,"
notes Mary Zubricky.

10 cups raw bulgur wheat
3 pints cherry tomatoes
2 cups minced fresh parsley
4 cups thinly sliced scallions, including green tops
2 tablespoons chopped fresh mint
or 1 tablespoons dried
1 1/4 cups lemon juice
3 cups olive oil
salt and pepper to taste

Place bulgur wheat in a very large bowl. Cover with boiling water, let stand 30 minutes or until tender. Drain well. Add remaining ingredients, mix to blend well.

Cover and chill at least 2 hours or up to 48 hours.

Yvonne Steinbring's BROCCOLI SALAD
Serves 18 - 20

5 or 6 large stalks fresh broccoli
2 cups raisins
1/2 cup thinly sliced red onion
12 slices bacon, diced, fried and drained on paper towel
2 cups sunflower seeds

Dressing:
1/4 cup sugar
1 cup mayonnaise or salad dressing
1/4 cup vinegar

Wash broccoli. Cut off bottom of stalks and peel. Slice stalks and cut flowers into bite sized pieces. Put into salad bowl. Add raisins, onion, bacon and sunflower seeds.

Mix dressing ingredients and pour over salad. Mix lightly, cover and chill before serving. Can be made several hours ahead or night before.

YVONNE STEINBRING'S CAULIFLOWER SALAD
Serves 20 - 24

        2 large heads fresh cauliflower
        1 bunch (5 or 6) green onions, sliced (use some green, too)
        2 bunches radishes, sliced (save a few for garnish)

Dressing:
        2 cups cultured light sour cream
        2 cups mayonnaise or salad dressing
        2 packages dry salad dressing mix
                (cheese and garlic flavor is good).

Wash cauliflower and cut into bite-sized pieces. Put into large bowl. Add sliced onions and radishes.

Mix dressing ingredients and fold into vegetables. Garnish with reserved radishes. Chill.

Variation: Add a stalk or two of broccoli, cut into bite-sized pieces (peel and slice the stem) for more color.

CREAMY COLE SLAW
Serves 20 - 24
Barbara Taylor prepares this salad.

        4 quarts cabbage finely shredded
        1/4 cup sugar
        1/4 cup lemon juice
        1/4 cup salad dressing or mayonnaise
        1/4 cup light or table cream
        1/2 teaspoon salt and pepper

Place shredded cabbage in large bowl . Sprinkle with sugar.
Toss. Chill 30 minutes.

Mix remaining ingredients and pour over cabbage. Mix well.

MIXED GREEN SALAD
Yield: 2 1/2 gallons mixture 3/4 cup portions for 50
*"I found adding jacima, celery heart or water chestnuts gave the salad
a crisp, crunchy texture that we prefer," Jan Cozzalio states.*

2 1/2 pounds (2 quarts) coarsely shredded cabbage
4 heads or bunches (7 quarts) coarsely shredded greens*
1 large pepper (1/2 cup)
1 bunch thinly sliced celery (2 cups)
1 dozen chopped hard-cooked eggs
1 1/2 pounds (6 approx.) tomatoes cut in small wedges
2 1/2 cups French dressing

*Equal amounts of lettuce, chicory, romaine, and escarole, or
any combination of these greens, may be used, depending on
availability.

Combine cabbage, greens, green pepper, and celery. Mix
thoroughly.

Just before serving, add eggs, tomato wedges, and French
dressing. Toss lightly.

POTATO SALAD
Yield enough for approximately 50 people
*Thelma Davis writes, "This is a basic potato salad that the children
enjoy. The secret seems to be in using Best Food Mayonnaise."*

20 pounds of potatoes
1 1/2 dozen eggs, hard-boiled
1 bunch celery (about 2 pounds), diced
2 medium onions, chopped fine
46 ounce sweet pickles, diced
2-3 tablespoons granulated sugar
1/4 cup dried parsley

4 ounces pimentos, chopped (optional)

Cook potatoes. Cool. Peel and dice potatoes. Add chopped eggs (or mash with potato masher, the children prefer them mashed) with celery, pickles, onions.

Blend all ingredients together with 48 ounces Best Food Mayonnaise. (May need more mayonnaise. Often I add a small amount of mustard to the mayonnaise depending on the potatoes.) Salt and pepper to taste. Serve chilled.

MINUTE RICE CHICKEN SALAD
Yields: 2 gallons - 5/8 cup portions for 50
Jan Cozzalio states, "This is really fast and easy. With a simple dessert and rolls it makes a very satisfying and complete luncheon."

> 3 5 ounce packages of Minute Rice
> 1 1/2 quarts water
> 2 1/4 teaspoons salt
> 1 1/2 quarts mayonnaise
> 2 tablespoons lemon juice (1 lemon)
> 2 4 ounce cans pimento
> 2 tablespoons salt
> 1 1/2 teaspoon pepper
> 5 12 ounce packages frozen peas (2 1/2 quarts)
> 3 5 pounds diced cooked chicken (2 1/4 quarts meat)
> 5 bunches diced celery (2 1/4 quarts)

Combine Minute Rice, water and salt in saucepan and cook as directed on the package for extra-tender rice. Keep covered and allow to cool to room temperature.

Mix together mayonnaise, lemon juice, pimento, and seasoning.

Add cooked rice, peas, chicken, and celery to mayonnaise mixture; toss together lightly.

Chill about 1 hour before serving. Serve on crisp lettuce with tomato slices, green pepper rings, or radish roses.

CRABMEAT SALAD
Use above recipe, substituting 2 1/2 quarts shredded crabmeat (six 6-ounce cans) for the chicken. Increase the lemon juice to 3 tablespoons.

Taco Salad
Serves 20

Linda (Grein) Barcus writes, "I have taken this to several family reunions and it has always been a hit. Place everything in a large bowl except for meat sauce and chips. Take the meat sauce in either a crock pot or insulated hot bowl, pour over cheese just before serving. Always have taco sauce setting next to the bowl for those brave enough to make it spicier."

2 pounds hamburger, cooked and crumbled
1 package taco seasoning
2 large packages shredded cheese
    (taco flavor or cheddar)
1 or more onions, chopped
2 or more tomatoes, chopped
1 large head of lettuce, chopped in small pieces
1 large package Doritos, crumbled
1 large bottle of Catalina dressing (or Western French)
Bottles of taco sauce

Brown hamburger, drain, and add taco seasoning following directions on package.

In large bowl place in layers as follows: Chopped lettuce, onions, tomatoes, cheese. Just before serving, pour hot hamburger over cheese. Let set a couple of minutes to melt cheese, pour dressing over meat sauce, top with crumbled Doritos. Toss together until well mixed. Serve.

Corn Casserole
Serves 10 - 12
Cleo Antoine is constantly asked to prepare this dish.

1 can mexi-corn
1 6 ounce package yellow rice
1 can cream of chicken soup
2 cups chicken, cooked & chopped
1 cup cheese, grated
3/4 cup crackers, buttered and crumbled
    (optional)

Cook rice according to directions.

Then mix everything together. Pour into casserole. Cover top with grated cheese and optional cracker crumbs to make it crunching.

Bake 350 degree until bubbly.

CHILI BEANS
Makes 64 cups
"The children at school enjoy these," states Thelma Davis

Wash 16 cups of dried pinto beans thoroughly the night before. Drain. Cover beans until the water is three inches above the beans. Soak overnight.

The next morning using the same water simmer beans with:

> 1 cup dehydrated onion
> 1/2 scant cup salt
> 1/4 cup ground cumin
> 1/4 cup chili powder
> 3 tablespoons garlic powder

When beans are half way cooked (about 1 1/2 hours at sea level)
> Add:

> 6 pounds ground beef, browned
> 4 cups tomato paste
> 2 cups catchup
> 4 cups canned tomatoes

Simmer 10 minutes then add to the beans.

Cook until soft. Season to taste.

CROCKPOT BEANS

"This is my most requested dish, and recipe. It makes a gallon, which
can serve a family as a main dish, or a group as a side-dish."
Jan Cowardin continues, "It gets better each time it is reheated, but
seldom is there enough left to reheat."

1 1/2 pounds hamburger, browned
1/2 pounds bacon, cooked and crumbled
1 white onion, chopped
32 ounce can of red kidney beans
32 ounce can of butter beans
64 ounces of pork 'n beans
2 cups catsup
1/3 cup vinegar, light
1/2 cup brown sugar
2 Tablespoons. liquid smoke
sliced mushrooms to taste

Cook all on high for 2 hours, then reduce heat to low and
continue cooking for 5 to 6 hours.

RANCH STYLE BAKED BEANS
Serves 16 - 20
Barbara Taylor makes these for their family gatherings.

4 tablespoons butter or margarine
2 pounds ground chuck
2 envelope dried onion soup mix
4 1 pound cans pork and beans in tomato sauce
2 large cans dark red kidney beans
2 cups catsup
1 cup cold water
4 tablespoons prepared mustard
4 cups cider vinegar

Preheat oven to 400 degrees. In large skillet melt butter or
margarine and brown meat. Stir in soup mix, beans, catsup,
water and vinegar. Pour into a 4 quart casserole or bean pot.
Bake 30 - 45 minutes or until hot and bubbly.

STUFFED CABBAGE
Serves 30

Mary Zubricky's mother taught her to make this dish when she was just a girl. "My mother was given this recipe by her Mother-in-law, who brought it with her from Yugoslavia when she came as a young bride. It has long been a favorite at family parties."

> 2 large heads cabbage
> 5 pounds ground chuck
> 2 1/2 cups long grain white rice, raw
> 2 large onions, minced
> salt and paper to taste
> 1 cup bread crumbs
> 5 eggs
> 3 48 ounce cans of tomato juice
> sour cream (optional)

Remove cores from cabbages and steam approximately an hour or until tender. Allow to cool until comfortable to handle.

Meanwhile, make filling. Mix remaining ingredients except tomato juice and sour cream. Remove leaves from cabbages one at a time. Place about 1/4 cup of filling in center of each leaf. Fold over sides of leaves and roll up. Place in large baking pan. Pour tomato juice over all to cover tops of cabbage rolls.

Bake at 350 degrees for about 2 hours. During baking, check to make sure there is enough juice remaining. Add more juice if liquid level is less than half the original amount. Serve with sour cream, if desired.

BEEF, FOWL, AND SEA-FOOD

BARBEQUED HAMBURGERS
Serves 50
Mary Zubricky writes, "This recipe came from an old family friend. It was one of my favorites at family gatherings when I was a child."

Hamburgers: 12 pounds ground beef
4 cups bread crumbs
6 eggs
3/4 cup milk

Mix well, shape into patties, brown on griddle. Place in large baking pans.

Barbeque sauce:

3/4 cup salad oil

2 1/4 cups chopped onion
1/2 cup catsup
2 15 ounce cans tomato sauce
2/3 cup lemon juice
1/2 cup brown sugar, packed
1/2 cup Worcestershire sauce
1/3 cup mustard
2 tablespoon salt
1 1/2 teaspoon black pepper

Saute onion in oil until soft. Add remaining ingredients, simmer 20 minutes. Pour over burger patties in baking pans. Bake at 350 degrees about 30 minutes or until cooked through.

Serve on buns.

TEXAS HO-DOWN
Any Number
James Walker contributes this large group Barbeque treasurer.

First yu'all need a BBQ large enough to cook for a small army.

Take a fifty-five gallon drum, cut it in half, weld it together, put legs on it about 32" high.

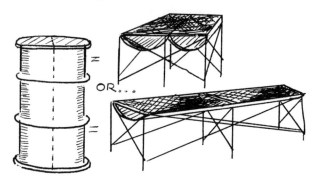

Add a piece of half inch crusher screen to the top. Now you got yourself a King size BBQ for about 200 folks.

Texas Top Sirloin, northern California style

Put about 25 - 30 pounds of briquets into each side of your fifty-five gallon drum, set them afire and let them burn down to a very hot bed of coals (about an hour give or take) while you prepare your meat.

What kind of meat do you want? Well sir, I suggest you buy Top Sirloin Butts. Each butt will weigh about 12 pounds average and feed about 20 - 24 hungry men, women and children.

Now you got it, how do you prepare it? Well sir, you take those butts and you trim off all the excess fat that you can. Cut them into large steaks. Vary the thickness from 1" to 2 1/4". By doing this when the meats cooked you will have a variety of meat rare to well done, something for everyone! Get yourself a large square cake pan, mix in it a mixture of two-thirds Lawreys Seasoning Salt to one-third Garlic Salt (if you want it cajun spicy add a little cayenne....but just a little). Take your steaks and roll then good in the seasoning until they have a thin crust of salt all over. Now they are ready for the BBQ.

Cooking Time

Make sure that your coals are good and hot. Throw that meat right on that hot grill and let 'er go to cook'n. Once it sears good on one side, flip it to the other and let it sear good on that side. Turn it often, don't worry about it getting black and look'n burnt, it ain't burnt on the inside. Let it cook for 20 - 30 minutes and check it with knife. Take it off when it looks good to you on the inside. Take those steaks when they're done and slice them into long thin strips about one-quarter inch thick. There, you're ready to serve .... hot delicious. Now chow down till you're ready to pop.

MY BARBECUE'S ARE THE PITS!

Ross Singleton is noted as the area's master pit barbecuer.

If you're looking for a quick and easy evening barbecue this is not the one for you! My style of pit barbecue requires lots of time and effort, but the rewards are just as great.

The place to start, naturally, is the pit. A pick and shovel won't do it, unless you have lots, I mean lots of time and energy...and help. A friend of mine with a backhoe came over to dig out a couple of tree stumps, so I persuaded him to dig a little hole about eight feet deep by six feet long and four feet wide. Your soil conditions will determine how much trouble you'll have and how big a pit you can dig. We only encountered clay with some small rocks.

Before you start digging the pit you should have located a source of rock averaging four to eight inches in diameter. These rocks will be used to fill the bottom two to two-and-one-half feet in the pit as a heat sink. We have an endless source of lava rock being near Mount Shasta, which may be the best kind of rock to use. Be careful about using river rock, as your Fourth of July party might start a little soon if the rocks start exploding, as commonly happens.

The next step should be to set forms and encase the pit from the lava rock in the bottom to the top with concrete, leaving the final inside dimensions of the pit about five-and-one-half feet deep, by three feet wide and five feet long. The concrete lining should be at least six inches thick. to cut down the amount of cement needed I used a lot of lava rock in the concrete sides. The rock also strengthened the concrete. Reinforcing steel is a good idea to prevent big slabs Cont'd pg. 162

RAVIOLI

Serves 20 or more

*Evelyn (Runnels) Fiock prepares this treat for special occasions
to the delight of everyone.*

Meat mixture:

Mix and put through grinder:

Half a loaf of bread soaked in milk.

1 large can of spinach, drained.

Mix thoroughly with above ingredients:

2 pounds hamburger

1 pound sausage

2 eggs

1/2 can grated parmesan cheese

1 onion, finely chopped

2 tablespoons salad oil

1/4 teaspoon ea: sage, thyme, marjoram, allspice

salt and pepper to taste

Dough:

6 eggs

6 egg-shell halves filled with water

6 cups flour

2 teaspoons salt

Mix as for noodles. Divide dough in quarters and roll into thin sheets. Drop teaspoons of meat mixture about 2 inches apart on half the rolled dough. Cover with other half of rolled dough. Press around each mound of filling with fingertips to form filled squares; cut squares apart with pastry cutter. (Or use ravioli equipment and use per manufacturers instructions.)

Sauce:

Small piece of boiling meat for flavor

1 onion, chopped

1 tablespoon parsley, chopped

5 cans hot sauce

salt and pepper to taste

1 teaspoon each: sage, marjoram, thyme,
cloves, allspice

celery stalks, few sliced

Bake in 350 degree oven 20 minutes to blend flavors.

Mix 1 can of American to 1/2 can grated parmesan cheese to sprinkle on individual servings.

In deep pot bring lightly salted water to rapid boil. Cook filled squares in the boiling water for about 10 minutes, or until the squares come to the top. Drain or remove carefully with slotted spoon.

Frequently this dish is served in individual portions to keep each ravioli whole. Top with sauce and a sprinkle of the cheese mixture. Evelyn says today she uses Prago sauce which "is certainly a lot easier to fix."

SWEDISH CHICKEN
Serves 20

"This recipe was given to me by a Swedish woman who spent ten days with our family one summer on a visiting teacher program. It quickly became a family favorite. I later adjusted the recipe to be served in a restaurant," Mary Zubricky said.

10 pounds chicken pieces
salt to taste
2 bunches fresh parsley
1 1/2 cups butter
4 cups heavy cream or Half-and-Half
2 Tablespoons. soy sauce

Wash and dry chicken pieces. Sprinkle lightly with salt. Melt butter in two or three large pots. Brown chicken pieces in butter on all sides. Add water to pots to a depth of about 1 1/2". Cover and simmer over low heat about 50 minutes until chicken is tender. Remove chicken to serving platters.

In one of the pots, whisk in 6 to 8 cups of flour to make a medium thick roux, gradually add cooking liquid from remaining pots. Whisk in cream and soy sauce, simmer gently until heated through. If gravy lumps (it can be difficult to make such a quantity) it can be processed in a blender or food processor to assure a smooth sauce. Pour over chicken and serve with boiled potatoes.

CHICKEN OR TURKEY TETRAZZINI
Serves 30 - 40

Linda (Grein) Barcus writes, " This is another make-ahead dish. Combine everything except for potato chips, place in casserole dish, cover and put in refrigerator or freezer. Before baking, place the chips on top. Could take up to an hour to warm through. This is great with left over turkey from the holidays. "

1 whole chicken (boiled and boned)
1 can Mushroom Soup
1 can Cream of Chicken Soup
1 can Cheddar Cheese Soup
1 can Celery soup
1 small jar Pimento
1 pound spaghetti
2 cups milk
1 package garlic flavored potato chips

Cook spaghetti, rinse and drain. In large sauce pan place all soups and milk, heat through. Combine warmed soups, spaghetti and chicken or turkey, pour in large casserole dish. Dot with butter, place crumbled potato chips on top, and bake at 350 degrees for 30-40 minutes.

BOUILLABAISSE
Serves 50

A Boy Scout Family Campout, years ago, prompted this version of a catch-of-the-day (with help from the local fish market) potluck. We had access to institutional size kettles and bowls, if you don't use smaller ones. It is a lot of fun, and smells oh-so good.

Stock:

12 pounds fish trimmings (head, skin and bones put into a cheesecloth sack)
3/4 cup olive oil
4 cups onions, chopped
8 stalks celery (leaves and all) chopped
8 carrots, sliced
12 sprigs parsley
2 teaspoons thyme

2 teaspoons rosemary
4 bay leaves
1 gallon water
2 quarts dry white wine

Wash the fish trimmings. Heat the oil in a 14 quart kettle. Add the vegetables and flavorings. Cook over low heat, stirring frequently, until onions are soft. Add the water, wine and fish trimmings. Bring to a boil and cook over medium heat for an hour and a half. Strain cheesecloth to abstract as much flavoring as possible. Some prefer to have the stock purely liquid and strain the remaining ingredients, others enjoy the 'chunks of vegetables'. Either way keep the stock hot.

Fish (or any combination of the-days-catch):
      12 pounds assorted sliced fish , 1/2 - 1 inch thick
          (rock fish should be scrubbed and scaled.
          Rockfish includes: lingcod, halibut, turbot, or
          sea bass)
      4 pounds squid, cleaned and coarsely chopped
      4 pounds eel, sliced
      8 1 1/2 pound lobsters, cut up and in shells
      50-100 clams in the shell, scrubbed clean
      8 crab legs in the shell, scrubbed clean
      4 pounds shrimp in the shell, scrubbed clean

Mix:
      1/4 cup salt
      2 teaspoons freshly ground pepper
      2 teaspoons thyme
      2 teaspoons rosemary
      2 teaspoons powdered saffron
      4 teaspoons fennel seeds, crushed
      1/2 cup olive oil

Pour the mixture over the washed and dried fish. Turn the fish combination to coat. Let stand 30 minutes.

In saucepan, over low heat, add:
      1/2 cup of olive oil
      2 bunches of thinly sliced green onion

Pour into the reserved boiling stock then add:
      the firmer pieces of fish, eel, squid, clams, lobster

> 1 1/2 quarts tomatoes, peeled and seeded
> 1 orange rind, sliced thin or shredded

Cover, bring back to simmering, and let cook gently until the clams pop open and the fish is no longer translucent in thickest part when prodded apart.

Bring to a boil, and cook over high heat for 5 minutes. Reduce heat to simmer, add the remaining fish and heat until mixture is heated throughout. Taste for seasoning.

While the fish is cooking prepare sauce:

> 8 cloves garlic, minced
> 2 teaspoons Tabasco
> 2 cups fresh bread crumbs, soaked and drained
> 1 cup olive oil
> 2 cups fish soup

Mix together the garlic, Tabasco, and bread crumbs; very gradually beat in the olive oil, then the soup.

When ready to serve, put a slice or two of dried bread in each deep soup bowl. Arrange the fish on a platter (or just dip in the kettle and enjoy what ever the dipper 'catches'). Serve the fish and soup simultaneously with a bowl of the sauce from which each person can help himself. (This is a modified Mediterranean style bouillabaisse.)

HOT CRAB CASSEROLE
Serves 10 - 12
This is another treasure from Cleo Antoine's collection.

10 slices white bread	4 eggs, beaten
2 cups crab meat	3 cups milk
1 cup celery, diced	1/2 cup mayonnaise
1 large onion, diced	1 cup mushroom soup
1 cup green pepper	1 cup sharp cheese, grated
2 tablespoons oil or margarine	
pepper to taste	

Saute celery, onion, and paper in oil. Remove crust from bread, cube 4 slices places in bottom of 9" X 13" X 2" pan.

Mix crab meat and vegetables with mayonnaise and spread over cubes. Place remaining bread slices over top (either cubed or whole). Beat eggs and milk together. Pour over bread mixture. Set in refrigerator over night.

Next day bake at 375 degrees for 15 minutes. Remove from oven and spoon soup over top with cheese.

Bake 1 hour at 350 degrees.

SHRIMP CREOLE WITH RICE
6 1/4 quarts shrimp creole, 7 quarts rice
1/2 cup portions serve 50
"A couple of my friends have used this group menu* for their gatherings and have always found it easy to prepare, and enjoyed by the quests," states Jan Cozzalio.

2 large chopped onions (1 1/2 cups)
1 bunch chopped celery (2 1/4 cups)
6 chopped green peppers (2 1/4 cups)
3 tablespoons salad oil or shortening
3 tablespoons flour
6 No. 2 cans tomato juice (3 1/4 quarts)
3 6 ounce cans tomato paste (1 1/2 cups)
2 tablespoons salt
1 teaspoon cinnamon
1 teaspoon nutmeg
1/2 teaspoon pepper
1/4 teaspoon cayenne
3 tablespoons lemon juice or vinegar (optional)
1/4 cup brown sugar (optional)
7 pounds fresh peeled cooked shrimp
(3 quarts/3 1/2 pounds)
10 5 ounce packages of Minute Rice

Saute onions, celery, and green pepper in oil or shortening until vegetables are browned.

Add flour and blend. Combine tomato juice, tomato paste,

* Fruit cup, Shrimp Creole with Rice**, Mixed Green Salad**, ice cream and coconut cake.

** Recipes in this group recipe section.

111

seasoning, lemon juice, and brown sugar. Add to vegetable mixture. Bring to a boil. Then reduce heat and simmer about 1/2 hour.

Add shrimp and continue cooking until mixture is heated through. Cook Minute Rice according to package directions.

Serve hot shrimp creole over rice.

Directions for cooking shrimp. Drop fresh shrimp (peeled or unpeeled) into 2 quarts briskly boiling salted water. Bring again to a boil, cover, and boil 3 to 5 minutes, or until shrimp is tender.

SEA FOOD GUMBO
Serves 12 to 14 large servings

Cleo Antoine writes, "When adding crab and shrimp you may add 1 pint oysters. I happen not to like oysters so I leave them out, unless requested otherwise. For variety you may also add one or more of: bacon, ham, cooked chicken (2 cups), or a good smoked sausage. Experiment with seasoning: rosemary, thyme. I always try a different one."

1 cup Wesson Oil
1 cup all purpose flour
2 cups celery, chopped
1 cup onion, chopped
1 bunch green onions, chopped (tops, too)
1 large green paper, chopped
2-3 cloves garlic, finely chopped

2 cups whole canned tomatoes, chopped
1 pound okra, sliced (frozen maybe used)
2-3 bay leaves
2 quarts water
2 tablespoons salt

5 pounds shrimp (heads off), peeled, de-veined
and washed
3 pounds crab meat (claws make best flavor)
3-4 drop hot sauce or red pepper flakes

In large Dutch oven heat oil using wooden spoon, add flour and cook to medium dark brown (DO NOT BURN) 30 to 45 minutes.

Stirring constantly add celery, onion and green onions, okra, green pepper and garlic - and cook additional 45 minutes. Cleo states, "You can shorten the cooking time here, however, the Gumbo isn't as good." Add broth, water, hot sauce, tomatoes and bay leaf and simmer 2 1/2 to 3 hours.

About 45 minutes to an hour before serving add shrimp, crab meat and claws. Serve over hot rice.

Note: You may use garlic salt or powder, also. Nine or ten chicken bullion cubes may be used instead of broth, however if using these check before adding more salt.

HU-MONGO HERO SANDWICH

*Bishop Probst states they have done this
at some of their gatherings and found it to be a winner.*

Check with your local bakery, or grocery store to find an oven that is large enough to bake the length of bread or loaf you desire. Probably the company will make and bake the bread for you, an alternate is to use french bread loaves sliced lengthwise (not quite as impressive but accomplished easier.) Decide what type of sandwich filling to use, gather the ingredients and proceed to make a major delectable sandwich. Be sure to be generous with the filling, more like an old fashioned Dagwood Sandwich.

Appoint someone to slice sandwich sections for the guests.

a different approach. One day when my husband was doing nothing in particular, I said, "Honey, I wish you'd teach me how to bake a cake."

He got out the flour, sugar, eggs, milk, shortening, chocolate and baking soda, but there was no sign of scratch. I watched him carefully blend it all together, poured it into a pan, then put it in the oven to bake. An hour later, when we were eating the cake, he couldn't understand my asking, "Honey, why don't we raise a few chickens?"

###

DESSERTS AND MORE

BANANA SPLIT CAKE
Serves 16 - 20
I like to serve this to groups who will eat it immediately.
It doesn't keep. Children of all ages like this sweet treat.

Combine: 2 cups graham cracker crumbs
                 1 cube melted butter
Mix thoroughly and spread into 9" X 13" X 2" pan.

Mix: 2 cups powdered sugar
                 2 eggs
                 1 cube softened butter
Beat until light and fluffy - spread over crumbs.

                 4 - 5 bananas sliced lengthwise
Place on top of spread.

                 1 large can of crushed pineapple, drained
Place on top of bananas then top with few more sliced bananas.

                 1 large thawed container Cool Whip

Spread on top. Decorate with slivered almonds and maraschino cherries.

BEST FRUIT CAKE EVER
Linda (Grein) Barcus writes, "Before beginning to mix recipe
read through first."

1 cup butter	1 tsp. salt
1 cup sugar	lemon juice
4 large eggs	1 cup brown sugar
1 tsp baking powder	nuts
1 tsp baking soda	1 or 2 quarts whiskey

Before you start, sample the whiskey to check for quality. Good, isn't it? Now go ahead. Select a large mixing bowl, measuring cup, etc. Check the whiskey again as it must be just right. To be sure the whiskey is of the highest quality, pour one level cup into a glass and drink it as fast as you can. Repeat. With an electric mixer, beat a cup of butter in a large fluffy bowl. Add one teaspoon of thugar and beat again. Meanwhile, to make sure that the whiskey is of the finest quality, cry another tup. Open second quart if necessary. Add 2 arge leggs, 2 cups fried druit and beat till high. If druit gets stuck in beaters, just pry it loose with a drewscriver. Sample the whiskey again, checking for tonscisticity. Then sift 3 cups of salt or anything, it really doesn't matter. Sample the whiskey. Sift 1/2 pint lemon juice. Fold in chopped butter and strained nuts. Add 1 babblespoon of brown thugar, or whatever color you can find, and mix well. Grease the oven and turn cake pan to 350 degrees. Now pour the whole mess into the coven and ake. Check the whiskey again, and go to bed.

DEVIL'S FOOD CAKE
Makes two 9'X12"X2" pans
Thelma Davis has prepared this so often- she has it memorized.

Cream till light:

        4 cups sugar
        1 1/2 cups butter

Sift:

        6 cups flour
        1 teaspoon salt
        6 tablespoons powdered buttermilk
        1/2 cup cocoa
        4 eggs, beaten.

Add to sugar mixture alternating between dry mix and:

        1 1/3 cups water + 1 tablespoon vanilla.

Beat until smooth.

Add:

        4 teaspoons baking soda to 2 cups boiling water and mix with other ingredients.

Bake at 350 degrees for 35 to 40 minutes.

THE BEST RHUBARB DESSERT
Serves 16 - 20

Yvonne Steinbring writes, "This recipe originally came from a church cookbook my sister had about 20 years ago. I use more rhubarb than the original recipe. If rhubarb is in season, this is a great addition to the menu. My mouth waters just thinking about it!"

Crust:

> 1 cup flour
> 1/2 cup butter
> 5 tablespoons powdered sugar

Combine as for pie crust; spread and press into 9" X 13" X 2" pan. Bake for 12 minutes at 350 degrees.

Filling:

> 3 eggs
> 1 1/2 cups sugar
> 1/4 cup flour
> 3/4 teaspoon baking powder
> 1 teaspoon vanilla
> 1/2 cup chopped nuts
> 4 - 6 cups diced rhubarb

Beat eggs. Add remaining ingredients. Put rhubarb on crust; pour filling over top. Bake at 350 degrees for 30 minutes. Cool.

Cut in squares to serve. May be topped with ice cream or whipped topping or cream.

YVONNE STEINBRING'S PUMPKIN RUM BREAD PUDDING
Serves 16

> 6 - 8 cups bread cubes (some whole wheat is good)
> 1/2 cup walnuts
> 1/2 cup raisins
> 3 eggs, slightly beaten
> 1 can (14 ounce) sweetened condensed milk

1 can canned pumpkin
1/2 cup packed brown sugar
2 teaspoons cinnamon
1/2 teaspoon nutmeg
2 cups milk
1/4 cup rum
1/4 cup butter or margarine, melted
2 teaspoons vanilla

Put bread cubes, raisins, and nuts in bottom of greased 12" X 7" X 2" baking pan.

Stir together: eggs, condensed milk, pumpkin, sugar and spices. Gradually stir in milk. Add rum, butter or margarine and vanilla. Pour over bread layer.

Place pan in larger baking pan (13" X 9" X 2"). Pour hot water into larger pan to 1 inch depth. Bake at 350 degrees for 50 - 60 minutes or until knife inserted off center comes out clean.

Serve warm or cold with whipped cream, if desired. Store in refrigerator.

Blushing Apple Pie
Serves 6
As I referred to this dessert on the sample label, am including it.

Make your favorite single pie crust, and line pie pan.

6 cups of peeled and sliced apples
1 (3 oz) package of strawberry gelatin
2 tablespoons sugar
1 cup sifted flour
1 cup sugar
1/2 cup butter

Lay apple slices on dough so they overlap.
Combine gelatin and 2 tablespoons sugar; sprinkle over apples.
Combine 1 cup flour and 1 cup sugar. Cut in 1/2 cup butter until coarse crumbs are formed. Sprinkle crumbs over apples.

Bake in 350 degree oven 50-60 minutes or until done. Serve with whipped cream, if desired.

CHEESE CANDY
6 pounds
Zelma Walter liked this recipe for groups and gifts.

1 pound margarine
1 pound Velveeta cheese
4 pounds powdered sugar
1 cup cocoa
1 teaspoon vanilla

Melt cheese and butter. Sift cocoa and powdered sugar. Add nuts and vanilla. Add cheese and butter. Spread in pan.

ALMOST-A-MEAL COOKIES
Makes 8 dozen 2" cookies, approximately
When my son was in second grade his teacher called and asked for my "Clean-The-Kitchen" recipe. I had no idea what she meant. After the mystery was solved I could see how a child might think these cookies were made of left-overs. It is an oatmeal cookie base that I add whatever fruits, nuts, and rice cereal available to make it hearty.

(Creaming is very important.)
Cream:

2 cups sugar
2 cups brown sugar, packed
2 cups softened margarine

When the sugars are fluffy, add:
4 eggs continue beating

Then:

4 cups Flintstones Fruity Pebbles
(or any rice cereal)
2 cups shredded coconut

Then: 2 teaspoons vanilla continue beating

Gradually add sifted flour mixture:

            4 cups flour
            2 teaspoons baking soda
            1 teaspoon salt

Add stirring by hand:

            4 cups quick cooking rolled oats
            1 1/2 cups raisins, currents, dried fruits cut-up
            1 cup of walnuts or various nut meats (optional)

Batter will be quite stiff. Drop batter by teaspoons onto a greased cookie sheet. Bake about 12 to 15 minutes in 350 degree oven.

DOUBLE BUTTER SCOTCH COOKIES
Makes 8 dozen 2" cookies approximately
Sterling Fiock, Robbie Hutchison and some of their
high school friends spent months developing this special cookie.

Cream until light and fluffy:

            2 cups softened margarine
            1 1/2 cups packed brown sugar
            1 1/2 cups sugar

Then add:

            4 eggs
            2 tablespoons vanilla

When well-creamed add the flour mixture a little at a time:

            2 cups flour
            2 teaspoons baking soda
            1 teaspoon cinnamon
            1 teaspoon salt
            3 1/2 ounce butterscotch instant pudding mix

Stir-in: 6 cups uncooked instant rolled oats
            1 package butterscotch chips

Drop by tablespoon onto ungreased cookie sheets. Cook in preheated oven 375 degrees for 8 minutes. Cookies will be puffy, LET *'SET'* A FEW SECONDS before moving to cooling racks. These cookies are chewie. Check a baked cookie to be sure the centers are done to your satisfaction.

Jan Cozzalio's
FORMULA TO SERVE 50

Bread (1 1/2 # loaf)	3 half slices	3 loaves
Butter	1.2 oz	1 1/2 #s
Cake	1 slice	4 large cakes
Coffee	1 6oz cup	1 # to 2 1/2 gal. water
Coffee, Instant	1 cup	2 2 oz jars - 10 qts water
Cream (coffee)	2 tablespoons	1 1/2 quarts
Cream (whipping)	1 tsp. (heaping)	1 quart
Sugar (coffee)	1 1/2 teaspoon	1 #
Sugar, cubed	1 lg. or 2 sm.	1 # lg, 1/2 # sm. cubes
Fruits, mixed (cup/salad)	1/3 - 1/2 cup	4 - 6 quarts
Ice Cream, bulk	8 per quart	6 1/2 quarts
Meat:		
Beef, Pot Roast, Round	3 1/2 oz cooked	18-20 #s
Beef, Standing Rib	3 1/2 oz cooked	20-25 #s
Chicken, for dishes	1 1/2 oz	13-17 #s drawn weight
		17-20 #s dressed weight
Chicken, roast	3 ozs	25-35 #s drawn weight
		35-50 #s dressed weight
Ground Meat, balls/loaf	1/5 #	12 #s
Roast Leg of Lamb	3 ozs	20-35 #s Variations in
		cooking & carving methods.
Turkey	3 ozs	20-25 #s drawn weight
		25-35 #s dressed weight
Pie	1/6	9 pies
Punch, fruit	3/4 cup	2 1/2 gal. - 1 cup ea.
Salad:		
vegetable, fish, chicken	1/2 cup	6 1/2 quarts
Salad dressing, garnish	1 tablespoons.	1 quart
Salad garnish; lettuce	1 lg leaf/2 sm	8 heads
Vegetables (canned)	1/2 cup	3 #10 cans
Vegetables (fresh)		
Asparagus	5 stalks (3 ozs)	12-16 #s
Beans, green or wax	3 ozs or 1/2 cup	10-12 #s
Cabbage, (cole slaw)	1/2 cup	14-16 #s (1# shredded = 2 qts)
Carrots	3 ozs or 1/2 cup	14-16 #s
Cauliflower	3 ozs or 1/2 cup	25 #s (56% waste, approx)
Peas	2 1/2 ozs	1/2 c 25 #s
Potatoes	2/3 cup	15 #s
Spinach	3 1/2 oz 1/2 c	15-17 #s
Tomatoes	5 per # sliced	10 #s fresh, sliced
		1 # = 2 cups diced
Vegetables, frozen		
Asparagus	3 ozs	13 boxes
Green or Wax Beans	3 ozs	13 boxes
Green Peas	3 ozs	13 boxes
Lima Beans	3 ozs	13 boxes

MEASUREMENT GUIDE*

LIQUID MEASURE CAPACITY

1 teaspoon   = 120 drops of water.
2 teaspoons   = 1 dessert spoon.
3 teaspoons   = 1 tablespoon.
1 tablespoon = 3 teaspoons.
2 tablespoons = 1 fluid ounce.
1 cup   = 16 tablespoons; 8 fluid ounces; 1/2 pint.
2 cups   = 1 pint.
1 pint   = 2 cups; 16 fluid ounces.
2 pints   = 1 quart.
1 quart   = 2 pints.
4 quarts   = 1 gallon.

APPROXIMATE FOOD WEIGHTS

1 pint measure of sugar   = 1 pound.
1 pint measure of butter   = 1 pound.
1 pint measure of lard   = 1 pound.
1 pint measure of flour   = 1/4 pound.
9 - 10 eggs   = 1 pound.
1 pint milk   = 1.075 pounds.
4 teaspoons baking powder   = 1 ounce
5 1/8 cups coffee   = 1 pound
6 1/2 cups tea   = 1 pound

* Based on information from The Household Encyclopedia, by N.H. and S. K. Mager, published by Pocket 1973.

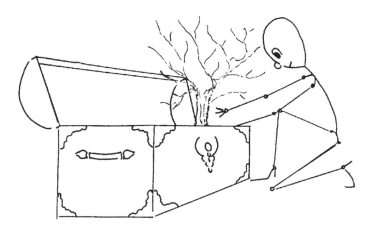

Genealogy

From idle curiosity to passion driven determination are the two extremes in the exploration of one's roots. Sometimes the idly curious can become overwhelmed with enthusiasm at a particularly "hot" lead. I know, it keeps happening. Genealogy is the research into one's ancestry, but as the poem (page xi) discovered in the Library of Congress questions, what would your ancestor's think of you? Interesting concept. The reason genealogy is so important in family reunions is: it allows us to understand our heritage; it gives a solid foundation to our family; and helps us locate living descendants from a common progenitor which is very important in some religions. This is an important, challenging and fun assignment, one which will continue for years.

Heraldry is the science of determining or settling a person's right to have a specific armorial bearing (coat-of-arms). Modern heraldry began in 1125-1150 A.D. using some symbols based in ancient cultures dating to 4000 B.C. Heraldry shops are scattered throughout the Nation in larger metropolitan cities. Many outlets have the more popular surnames on file with coat-of-arms decorations applied to practical as well as ornamental items; mugs, plaques, rings, door-knockers. In addition, they often offer a research service on the coat-of-arms, and family surname origins, and many note ancestors of exceptional accomplishments.

Gather factual information from your family. Explore family attics, trunks, basements and other areas where information might be kept. Family Bibles often list accurate birth and death dates, some even include where the individual was born, buried, to whom married, and their descendants. Go through the Bible carefully as often notes are made on scrape paper, stuffed into the Bible for future recording...which may not happen. Knowing the ancestor's religious preference helps but is not mandatory.

Old letters often reveal little known facts of a person's 'noblesse,' or personality. These tidbits give 'life' to factual information, and enrich the family 'promptbook'. Envelopes may bear postmarks, and dates to aid in your research.

Photograph albums are extremely valuable when the photographs are identified. However, don't despair if this is not the case in your family. Ask other family members. Eventually, most of the people will be identified. One of my favorite stories came from a lady whose husband had passed away while doing research on his family. She couldn't find anyone who knew the proud gentleman in a portrait. Deciding to gamble she sent the photograph to a genealogical society in Holland with a letter asking if anyone could identify the gentleman. The photograph roved about European genealogical societies for years. I think she told me it was seven years before she received a letter stating that the gentleman in the photograph was the author's great-uncle. The letter came from a small village in Germany.

"That," she added, "was some twenty years ago. I try to go the village at least every other year. They are such wonderful people. Indeed, they are my family, and have enriched my life so much. So don't ever throw away those unidentified photographs. You could be discarding relationships and years of happiness."

Family scrapbooks, even those compiled by children, journals, diaries and of course verbal and written histories are extremely important. State historical societies often have surname histories available. The Library of Congress has many family history books on file although self-published books are not required to be registered, however, many families send theirs for cataloguing.

Passports, certificates, announcements, invitations, newspaper clippings, citizenship papers, naturalization certificates and declarations of intent to become a citizen, are great sources. Memorial cards, wills, probates, land records, deeds, and mortgage papers are valuable tools. Report cards and other school memorabilia can depict a person's interest and moves.

Family traditions are an excellent method to determine a family's point of origin. Try to figure out what is meant when grandparents respond with, "That's just the way we do things." Try to trace which country has that particular custom. Family legends are an essential tool to tracing your heritage.

Enjoy pondering and exploring your family's unanswered questions. Follow every lead. Contact extended relatives, establish communication. Write to people with similar surnames. Often when people came to this country they did not know how to write or spell their surnames in English, so the interviewer simply wrote what he thought appeared probable. Some coun-

tries have titles woven in their surnames such as "van","'la",
and other similar titles were dropped when they came to the
United States. Some surnames reflect the native country,
location, occupation or interest of the family. Countries that
used a location as a surname in the old days can complicate
research as the name changed from location to location although
it was the same individual. A more commonly known fact is a
person's surname might reflect the individual's occupation;
"Smith" often referred to blacksmith. In some cultures children take the mother's name, while in others it is the father's
first name; Eric's son has varies spellings: Ericson, Ericsson,
Erickson, or a variation thereof. In this country a person can be
known by another name than the birth name as long as there is
no intent of fraud, or misrepresentation, which can further
complicate genealogical research.

Dates and places are vital in confirming information
and identification. Birth dates are especially important when a
family repeatedly uses the same first names. Places also are
instrumental in tracing lineage, but a country's boundaries may
change through the centuries while some cease to exist. The
further back you go in research the more changes you will
encounter, but that is part of genealogy's charm. That and the
excitement when a link is confirmed.

As you explore ancestral closets be careful of fragile,
old, tattered documents. To help preserve the documents wear
clean, white, cotton gloves or second best, plastic surgical
gloves. (Regular plastic gloves are too clumsy, and too risky to
have around such delicate material.) The old documents should
be kept flat, out of the direct sunlight, dry and in a moderately
cool atmosphere. Minimize folding and unfolding procedures.

Never write or draw extra lines on historic documents.

Some people try to 'restore' documents with home remedies, as a professional museum designer I beg you, don't. Take the treasures to a qualified frame studio that offers 'museum mounts'. There are papers, tapes and adhering agencies which are free of acids and other detrimental material to properly preserve pieces. This includes fabrics, too.

Many photo studios specialize in restoring old photographs. Ask to see samples of their work. Jim Ellis of Ceres, had an unfortunate experience when he gathered the families historic photos and delivered the group to a studio for reproduction and preservation measures. The studio burned. He suggests taking a few photographs in at a time.

Freys, a northern California family, suggest having duplicates made of all valuable photographs and give the copies to another family member in a different town or house. When their house burned all their family genealogical records, and photos were lost, too.

Tin types, glass negatives, and nitrocellulose film require special techniques to be developed into prints or positives. If you have any of these check with your closest university for a qualified developer in your area. Or contact me, I know a few people who develop these fragile documents. Be extremely careful with nitrocellulose film as this late 1800's film has a tendency to explode into flames.

Oral interviews can be true 'spell binders' as the story teller makes each incident live. There is a special talent for getting people to share their treasured memories, and experiences. An excellent book that may help is <u>From You To Your Ancestors.</u> One of the key things to remember when conducting oral interviews is ~ **listen**. Listening is in itself a real art, and a valuable asset in this application. For so many times, as people began to share they will completely withdraw if questioned unrealistically, or interrupted. Either use a recorder or keep accurate notes. To make the interview more creditable record the date, interviewee, and recommend that he use specific dates and locations when possible. We are programmed for a fairy tale when we hear "once upon a time." Just as you visualize their experiences so will others. This is a great way to help young family members become inspired by the everyday bravery and heroism that your ancestors endured to make our country what it is today. Perhaps you could share a specifically fascinating, active incident with the activities coordinator so it could be worked into a skit for the program.

Recording oral, or for that matter, written material that cannot be documented is difficult. Some people sincerely believe they are reporting the exact truth and would be offended if you questioned, definitely if you nitpick. When the information is detrimental to a person's integrity, trash cans make excellent file cabinets. Medical information and other serious concerns should be in a separate file, though. Quite often people interpret the same incident, room, conversation differently. For instance a debate between two gentlemen; One insisted the room was filled with mirrors, and had an impressive chandelier. The other just as stubbornly stated it was decorated with golden filagree on a glossy black wallpaper, and soft, flickering candlelight. After a lengthy debate they took their wives to the restaurant. Both were stunned to learn the other was right. It depended upon where one sat.

Therefore, as the family historian, file all information for future reference, unless it fits into the 'exception' category. It is much more important to keep everyone harmonious and inquisitive. Seldom do two people receive the same impression from an experience, even when it happened simultaneously. So how can we know the world our ancestor knew? There is an old adage that advises us not to judge another until we've walked a mile in their shoes.

There are pre-printed forms to aid the research process, two necessary forms are the Family Group and Pedigree / Ancestor Chart. The Family Group form pertains to a specific family unit. Pedigree or ancestor chart records both sides of an individual's ancestry for four or more generations. When the information can be substantiated, do so. Photocopies work well, just be sure to keep track of how and where the information was obtained.

The Siskiyou County Fiock family uses a promptbook concept to share gathered information. The Family Group chart information was transferred into a computer genealogical program (discussed in the following paragraph), printed, and placed into a ledger format. This book is taken to family gatherings where photographs, stories, and other information is added. It is a working scrapbook that lives up to its name of 'prompt' book. Everyone seems to take pride in contributing a photograph, or a story of their beloved ancestor. In time, there should be enough information and photographs to make an interesting family book. One member suggested including the current owner of various family heirlooms. On one hand this seems like a marvelous suggestion, but upon closer scrutiny it might be a potential hazard. Evaluate your own family to determine if this is applicable for you.

From experience it is strongly recommended that people understand information given to you or the executive board becomes accessible to all family members, unless specified otherwise.

Computers have made maintaining genealogical facts

much easier. There are numerous software programs available for MS-DOS and IBM formats. Macintosh and some other computers have less options. The type of computer will determine which software programs are available to you. If you are purchasing or upgrading a computer system, investigate the wide variety of genealogical software packages available. Then find the computer which will operate the software programs that meet your needs. Gen-N-Dex[8] is a mail order company that is dedicated to having books, supplies, softwear, computer systems, services, and family association and reunion articles. "Public Domain Software," which is software available to the general public free or for a nominal charge, has beginning genealogical research programs.

One of the most outstanding organizations in tracing ancestors is the Church of Jesus Christ of Latter Day Saints which welcomes non-Mormon explorations, too. Their genealogical library in Salt Lake City, Utah, probably holds the most extensive collection in the world. This massive collection has been accumulated over years, in part through their extraction program. Countries that need to ensure their vital records can send the original to this library. The genealogical library copies the original, returns the original with a copy to its country of origin, and retains a copy for their records.

Branch libraries are scattered throughout the world, and fairly accessible in the United States. I have found the librarians to be very helpful, friendly and enthusiastic to help a questioning novice. They explain how to use the microfilm, micofiche and many of their other index sources. One of those is the Family Registry system which networks individuals working on the

---

[8] Gen-N-Dex, P.O. Box 3684, Richmond, VA 23235 (804) 272-4875

same surname.

In conjunction with this extensive network is a publishing company known as Everton Publishers, Inc[9]. They have Family Group, Ancestor Charts, and numerous how-to books. Other helpful guides including: <u>Handy Book For Genealogists</u>[10]; <u>From You To Your Ancestors</u>[11]. The United States Printing Office in Washington[12], D.C. recommends writing for their publications addressed to the beginning genealogists: <u>Where To Write For Birth And Death Records</u>, and <u>Where To Write For Marriage Records</u>.

Well, now that all the business of genealogy has been taken care of here are some special touches for your reunion, and family.

The first is receiving a greeting card from the White House[13]. These are available for 50th wedding anniversaries, and 80th birthdays. In addition to a card sometimes a photograph of the President is available, when requested. To receive these write for a (number and occasion) card for (Uncle John) on (June 21). Please send the card and photograph to: (his address). Be sure to put your name, address and phone number on the requesting letter, in case they need to contact you.

Scott Willard, NBC-TV weatherman, recognizes centenarians weekdays on the Good Morning Show[14].

Locating biological parents or adopted children may be made easier through some national organizations. There are more than four million American-born adoptees in the United States. To answer the search of family seeking family members

[9] Everton Publishers, Inc., P.O. Box 368, Logan, Utah 84321
[10] Handy Book For Genealogists, P.O. Box 368, Logan, Utah 84321
[11] Genealogical Library, 50 E.N. Temple, Salt Lake City, Utah 84150
[12] U.S. Printing Office, Washington, D.C. 20402
[13] Greeting Office, White House, Room 39, Washington, D.C. 20500
[14] NBC-TV, Good Morning America, Scott Willard

there are more than 380 search and support groups across the country. Twenty-six states have reunion registries. Forty-eight states have sealed adoption records, however People Searching News[15] editor, Jone Carlson, states "Even so there have been many successful cases." PSN[15], a reference magazine for adoption issues and adoption searches. The group provides search help, a Search Kit ($8.00) includes forms and information to aid you in your search. Their 24-hour hotline is 305 370-7100.

The Adoptees' Liberty Movement Association[16] helps adoptees and their birth parents meet. The International Soundex Reunion Registry[17] is a mutual consent, no-fee reunion registry. Parties who sign the registry must be 18 years of age or older. When requesting a registration form, submit a business sized self-address, stamped envelope.

Patriotic and hereditary societies keep records of ancestors and their descendants. The U.S. Lineage Societies Register[18] lists these organizations. Three of the largest are: National Society of Daughters of the American Revolution[18a], National Society, United States Daughters of 1812[18b], and Sons of the American Revolution[18c].

Climbing the family tree is challenging;
you meet interesting people, and sometimes they're family!

[15] People Searching News, P.O. Box 22611, Fort Lauderdale, FL33335
    (305) 763-1162
[16] ALMA, P.O. Box 154, Washington Bridge Station, N.Y. 10033
    (212) 581-1568
[17] ISRR, P.O. Box 2312, Carson City, Nevada 89702-2312
[18] The U.S. Lineage Societies Register (FHL 973 C43r; fiche 6050647)
[18a] National Society of the Daughters of the American Revolution,
    1776 D St NW, Washington, D.C. 20006
[18b] National Society, United States Daughters of 1812,
    1461 Rhode Island Ave. NW, Washington, D.C. 20005
[18c] Sons of the American Revolution, 1000 South Fourth St.,
    Louisville, KY 40203

RELATIONSHIP CHART

G Father=grandfather; gg father =great grandfather; unc=uncle; bro=brother; c & cou =cousin; neph=nephew; r=generations removed

		1 COU	2 COU	3 COU	4 COU
3GGFATHER (3gg son)					3GG UNC (3 gg neph)
GGFATHER (2 gg son)				GG UNC (2gg neph)	1c3r
GFATHER (g son)			G UNC (g neph)	1c2r	1c2r
FATHER (son)		UNC (neph)	1c1r	2c1r	3c1r
SELF — BRO		1 COU	2 COU	3 COU	4 COU
SON (father) — NEPHEW (uncle)		1c1r	2c1r	3c1r	4c1r
G.SON (g father) — G NEPHEW (g unc)		1c2r	2c2r	3c2r	4c2r
GG SON (gg father) - GG NEPHEW (gg unc)		1c3r	2c3r	3c3r	4c3r

FAMILY GROUP *(sample, actual form 8-1/2x11)*

Information Sources:

Husband's Full Nam

Husband's		
Data	Day Month Year	City,
Birth		
Chr'nd		
Mar.		
death		
Burial		
Places of Residence		
Occupation		
Special Interests and Hobbies		
List other wives, if any. Starting with first each wife should be supported with a sepa		
His Father		

Wife's Full Maiden N

Wife's		
Data	Day Month Year	City,
Birth		
Chr'nd		
Mar.		
Death		
Burial		
Places of Residence		
Occupation		
Special Interests and Hobbies		
List other husbands, if any. Starting with f Each should be supported with a separate		
Her Father		

Children's Data

Sex	Children's Name in Full Arrange in order of birth.		Day Month Year	City, Town or
		Birth		
		Mar.		
Full Name of Spouse		Death		
		Burial		
		Birth		
		Mar.		
Full Name of Spouse		Death		
		Burial		

134

e

Town or Place	County or Province, etc.	State or Country	Add. Info.

Religious Affiliation	Military Record

wife, second etc.
irate family group sheet.

Mother's Maiden Name

Jame

Town or Place	County or Province, etc.	State or Country	Add. Info.

Religious Affiliation	Military Record

irst, second etc·
family group sheet.

Mother's Maiden Name

Place	County or Province, etc.	State or Country	Add. Info.

ANCESTOR CHART *(sample, actual form 8-1/2X11)*

Chart No._____

Compiler _____
Address _____
City, State _____
Date _____

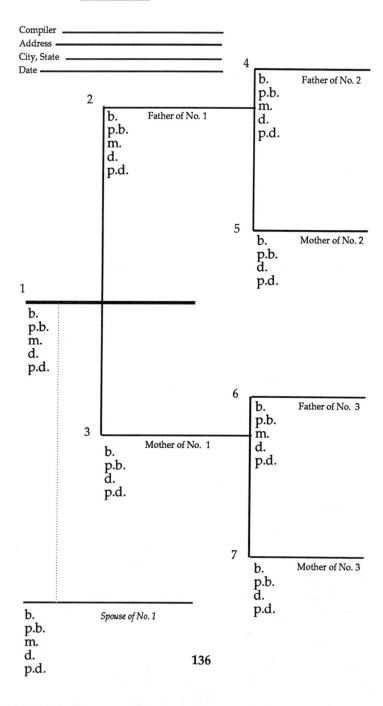

4

b.   Father of No. 2
p.b.
m.
d.
p.d.

2

b.   Father of No. 1
p.b.
m.
d.
p.d.

5

b.   Mother of No. 2
p.b.
d.
p.d.

1

b.
p.b.
m.
d.
p.d.

6

b.   Father of No. 3
p.b.
m.
d.
p.d.

3

b.   Mother of No. 1
p.b.
d.
p.d.

7

b.   Mother of No. 3
p.b.
d.
p.d.

b.   *Spouse of No. 1*
p.b.
m.
d.
p.d.

136

FAMILY LIFE

No. 1 on this chart is the same person as No. _____ on chart No. _____.

b.=Date of Birth, p.b.=Place of Birth, m.=Date of Marriage, d.=Date of Death, p.d.=Place of Death.

16

b. | Father of No. 8,
m. | cont. on chart no. _____
d.

8

b.
p.b. | Father of No. 4
m. | **17**
d.
p.d. | b. | Mother of No. 8,
| d. | cont. on chart no. _____

9 | **18**

b. | Father of No. 9,
m. | cont. on chart no. _____
d.

b.
p.b. | Mother of No. 4
d. | **19**
p.d. | b. | Mother of No. 9,
| d. | cont. on chart no. _____

20

b. | Father of No. 10,
m. | cont. on chart no. _____
d.

10

b.
p.b. | Father of No. 5
m. | **21**
d.
p.d. | b. | Mother of No. 10,
| d. | cont. on chart no. _____

11 | **22**

b. | Father of No. 11,
m. | cont. on chart no. _____
d.

b.
p.b. | Mother of No. 5
d. | **23**
p.d. | b. | Mother of No.11,
| d. | cont. on chart no. _____

24

b. | Father of No.12,
m. | cont. on chart no. _____
d.

12

b.
p.b. | Father of No. 6
m. | **25**
d.
p.d. | b. | Mother of No. 12,
| d. | cont. on chart no. _____

13 | **26**

b. | Father of No. 13,
m. | cont. on chart no. _____
d.

b.
p.b. | Mother of No. 6
d. | **27**
p.d. | b. | Mother of No. 13,
| d. | cont. on chart no. _____

28

b. | Father of No. 14,
m. | cont. on chart no. _____
d.

14

b.
p.b. | Father of No. 7
m. | **29**
d.
p.d. | b. | Mother of No. 14,
| d. | cont. on chart no. _____

30

b. | Father of No. 15,
m. | cont. on chart no. _____
d.

15

b.
p.b. | Mother of No. 7
d. | **31**
| b. | Mother of No. 15,
137 | d. | cont. on chart no. _____

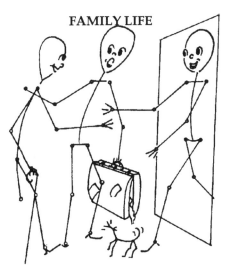

Host/Hostess

Coordinating travel plans to little known areas can be confusing. The host/hostess can help make arrangements by gathering information where family members can stay. At commercial sites such as hotels, motels and resorts, group rates are often available which can stimulate communication between family members. Perhaps a better method to develop communication between families is having families stay with another family unit. This takes a little effort to be certain personalities and interests are similar. In addition, note assets, such as well lighted, no stairs, wheelchair facilities and children okay. When matching families, listen for the special needs of both families.

Many states have restraint laws that require approved car seats for children. Short term use infant car seats are often available through a service organization, check with the chamber of commerce to see if this is an option in your area. If not, rental companies probably have children's car seats available. Pharmacies frequently have medical equipment (wheel chairs, oxygen tanks) for rent.

Cross check with each family before making confirmations. Encourage families to exchange identification photographs before meeting at a commercial transportation facility.

Not all families will need a host/hostess, as the president or executive board can coordinate infrequent requests. However, for extremely large families it can be helpful.

Master of Ceremonies or Program

Washington Irving scribed, "Honest good humor is the oil and wine of a merry meeting, and there is no jovial companionship equal to that where the jokes are rather small and the laughter abundant." Sounds like a good formula for the master of ceremonies of a family reunion.

Family programs which portray family heritage through skits, music, or songs, in addition to having a speaker present an anecdote or family history, are excellent. The people or groups who take part in the program should have ample time to prepare and practice, which may take weeks for skits and dances.

After introducing various individuals who take an active role in the program, recognize the oldest, the youngest, most recently married, traveled the farthest, and other recognition categories. Perhaps the activities coordinator can acknowledge sport winners with inexpensive trophies. Make announcements, review the remaining itinerary. The coordinator will thank the executive board, the committee workers, and all who made the event a success.

To achieve your goal of making it a, "Thank goodness I

came" memory the program must reflect flexibility, wit, humor and be easily heard. Amplifiers, overhead projectors, camcorders, and VCRs can add interest to a program, and should be readied for use before the program.

The Koch family of Pennsylvania celebrate each sibling's birthdays with the celebratee acting as master of ceremonies on his special day. Carole writes, "As children we were too poor to recognize birthdays, so now we are making up for it." The family meets at the master of ceremonies' (birthday person) choice and dictates the festivities which can range from cocktail to costume parties. Sounds fun for small groups.

IMPORTANT:

Welcoming the captive audience, then make them comfortable with a brief joke. Introduce the performer(s) with a complement. Be sure to thank the performer(s) for the presentation. Make a stimulating comment for the next performer. Keep the program flowing smoothly from one performance to another.

Achieve an upbeat mood
with lots of
laughter and comaraderie
with the audience.

Photographers

Oh, the clicking of the cameras and whirring of the camcorders will be prolific...probably within a certain familiar family branch. It is understandably difficult to take pictures of people one barely knows, therefore assigning a family member as the 'official' photographer is a good option.   This person can circulate among families taking candid shots for distribution through the clan.

Family unit or group pictures are another valuable asset an 'official' photographer can arrange. These photographs are a fine addition to promptbooks, aid newly united clans in identifying family units, and are an excellent record of family changes. Families with young children may want their group photographs taken before children get dirty.   Not all family units will cooperate, which prompted a recommendation for the photographer to issue a 'ticket' as each family unit is photographed. The 'ticket' could be 'cashed' at the food line. Interesting concept. If you try it please let me know how it worked, I am not brave enough to try it in our family.

Family groups of four, five or six generations definitely

should be photographed. Many local newspapers are interested in this type of photograph, which can make an excellent lead-in for a press release. Family records can be enhanced with portrait photographs of the eighty plus year olds.

Large group photographs are difficult to take, and often individual faces are too small to identify. There are special cameras that help in borderline large groups. At our last reunion we tried the wide angle disposable camera; however, the image is too dark and not usable. To show group attendance take candid over-all shots of various activities.

The most efficient way to distribute photographs is to develop them each evening or at least the day before the final event. (Many places offer one hour developing services for prints. Slides, and black and white print film takes longer.) Family units can than make and pay for their print selections. (Be sure to charge enough to cover your expenses for the film development, chipboard[19], envelopes, and postage.) One family had everyone send their photographs to a mutual collection which was mailed to each family unit. The process was difficult to manage, and extremely expensive due to the numerous long distance phone calls to keep the collection moving.

Ordering procedures are fairly standard. The developed roll will be returned with negative strips. The negative strips have an identification number near each frame. To order match the print to the negative strip, make note of the identification frame number. Studio envelopes usually have a box with numerous smaller numbered boxes inside. These numbered boxes correspond to the negative strip numbers, write the number of prints desired in the corresponding box. DO NOT

---

[19] Chipboard is a thin piece of cardboard available at most printing shops.

CUT THE NEGATIVES APART. Be sure to keep the negative

SPECIFY NUMBER OF PRINTS OR ENLARGEMENTS DESIRED OPPOSI
NEGATIVE NUMBER.   *IMPORTANT: PLEASE DO NOT CUT NEGATIVI*

FOR REGULAR PRINTS

00	00A	12	12A	25	25A
0	0A	13	13A	26	26A
1	1A	14	14A	27	27A
2	2A	15	15A	28	28A
3	3A	16	16A	29	29A
4	4A	17	17A	30	30A
5	5A	18	18A	31	31A
6	6A	19	19A	32	32A
7	7A	20	20A	33	33A
8	8A	21	21A	34	34A
9	9A	22	22A	35	35A
10	10A	23	23A	36	36A
11	11A	24	24A	37	37A

FOR ENLARGEMENTS

NEG NO	QUAN	SIZE

SPECIAL INSTRUCTIONS

strips with the appropriate film roll group.   Insert a piece of
'chipboard' the same size as the envelope to keep the photographs
from damage.   Mark on front of the envelope, "PHOTOS DO
NOT BEND."

Identifying the prints from the negatives can be a difficult task, but made easier with the use of a light table.   When I
started our business in 1968 I made a 'light box' from a cardboard
box.   The original box should be sturdy and have a lid, and be
at least six inches deep by eighteen inches square.   Cut the box
per the diagram, line with heavy duty aluminum foil before

adding a 25 (maximum 40) watt
light bulb and socket to the center
in the six inches deep back.   Non-
glare plexiglass or frosted glass top
will diffuse the light so the negative
strips can be viewed easier.   The

box is not intended for long periods of use, and should be
unplugged when not in use.

**This is a fun position, one which utilizes
photography, communication, and public relation skills.**

(PRE-REGISTRATION FORM sample)

ADVANCE REGISTRATION

Name: _____ Date _____

Address _____

Phone # (day) _____ (night) _____

We want to show our _____

it will need an area approximately: _____

Special considerations: (weight/or other exhibit concerns) _____

___ Yes! We can help. Please let us know how. ___Unable to now.

We would like to volunteer to: _____

_____ is a musician, dancer, comedian, historian, and would like to participate in the program.

ITEM	WHEN	COST EA.	# Child/Adult	COST
Activity				
Activity				
REUNION				

TOTAL ENCLOSED.................$_____

Children discounts are 12 and under. There is no senior citizen discount.
FAMILY REUNION COMMITTEE
ADDRESS
(Date)

The back side of this card is for the treasurer, historian, genealogist, coordinator, etc to leave messages or comments.

Registration

Part of making a "Thank goodness I came" event is the smooth flowing of all activities. That begins with a warm welcome upon entering. To facilitate that use a registration form. There are two types, one is the basic family unit registration card, while the other includes interests, payment, and extra activity participation with the back side used for notes from various committees. Most families find the latter form better with its first record being entered by the treasurer after receiving the family units check, and dispersing it accordingly.

Set the table near the main entrance where registration forms, and name tags can be easily disbursed. As means of stimulating togetherness ask them to put an adhesive dot next to their name on the large graphic family tree (if you have one). As everyone will register at this site it can be a good location for your beloved senior citizens or guest of honor.

List activities and other functions on a blackboard which can be easily read while people register. If your group is very large, and the event will cover a few days, use the blackboard for messages and other communiques. In many cases the grapevine is sufficient.

As the event's receptionist
you set the mood for the event,
so be sure everyone receives a sincere and warm welcome.

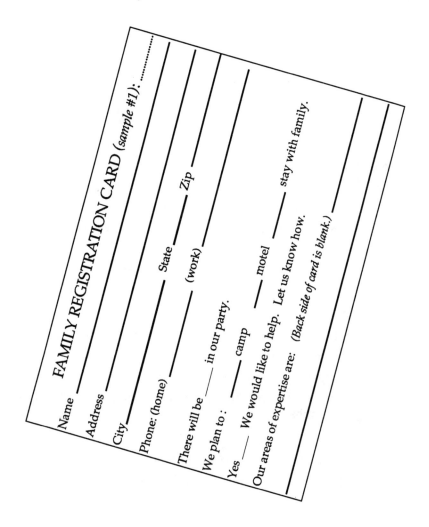

FAMILY REGISTRATION CARD (sample #1): ....

Name _____

Address _____

City _____ State _____ Zip _____

Phone: (home) _____ (work) _____

There will be ____ in our party.

We plan to : ____ camp ____ motel ____ stay with family.

Yes ____ We would like to help. Let us know how.

Our areas of expertise are: (Back side of card is blank.)

Security

No offense is intended, but when another sees a beloved's item in the possession of another, anything can happen. By developing a specified area where heirlooms can be safely viewed, much like a museum, it offers comfort to those showing heirlooms. This area is especially nice for clan gatherings, but may be inappropriate for reunions where sharing is more personal. A tent or gazebo can work nicely as a viewing area. Tents or awnings will not damage the lawn if they are up for a short period of time (a day or so).

Try to display the items to their best advantage. Photo collages make group photographs more interesting. Simply by putting an odd number of photographs together with one acting as the focal point. Mixing black and white photographs with colored photographs in a collage can be challenging, but is not impossible. Experiment by adding colored paper or fabric behind the black and white one, or behind the group. Another inexpensive option is the use of space...blank empty space.

Some paintings can be displayed on an artist's easels, tripods or other similar stands. Other 'hangable' items can easily be hung on peg-board frames. It's advisable to brace a four-by-eight feet plywood sheet on top, bottom and in the center. Necklaces and other small items can be made more secure by draping a clear sheet of plastic over the entire exhibit. For items viewed on a table use clear plastic sheet to offer protection. Chairs, cradles and similar items should have a ribbon tied across them to deter use. Restored automobiles, carriages and similar items should stay in the parking lot in a roped off area.

Identification tags add a great deal to the exhibit. Of course, having courteous, knowledgeable family historians elaborate on the exhibits adds greatly to the overall success of the 'family' museum.

Make certain exhibitors understand that sharing is done at their own risk.

Ahh, the reminiscing
this activity will bring,
and the pride of younger family members
upon being able to bring their ancestors to 'life'.

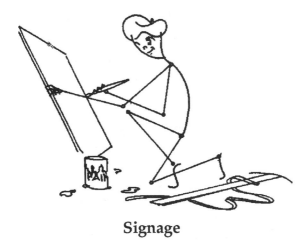

Signage

Part of achieving the "Thank goodness I came" memory is making everyone comfortable. Visual communiques such as name tags, identification labels, graphic family tree, and similar signage helps. One activity that should be started well before the event is designing the family tree.

After years of organizing projects I find color coding one of the easiest. Select a color for the progenitor's children and write one child's name per label. It is necessary to use a product that can be easily rearranged. Pre-gummed address labels work well on the waxed paper, or use removable artist's scotch tapes. Arrange the labels on a large waxed sheet of paper, if it won't take too long, press-on tags work. Take another color and repeat the process through all the generations. Some families state they included the full given name, birth and death dates, it may be an extra step if the information is kept in a promptbook.

Keep an accurate legend in one of the corners. Assign each color a generation, each symbol a meaning. Develop a code such as a diagonal line before a name to indicate maiden name unknown, whereas a diagonal line after a person's name might indicate a divorce. In multiple marriages and various step-children the process becomes a little complicated. Step-children of a divorced spouse are not always shown, unless the children were raised in the family nucleus. However, bloodline and adopted children should always be listed. When a marriage was short lived, and no children were born to the union, it is optional information for the family graphic tree.

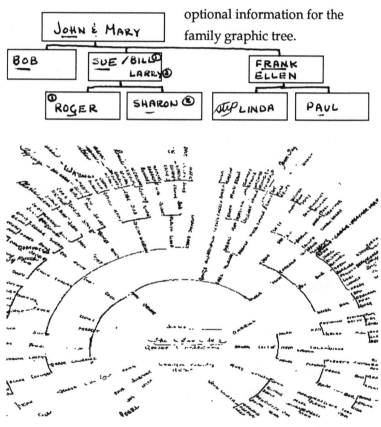

Once all the family members are represented experiment with making a permanent large graphic family tree on plywood or fabric. I tried a number of formulas but found starting with the progenitor at the base and working out like a tree best.

In sample A, the Meamber family used a full sheet of

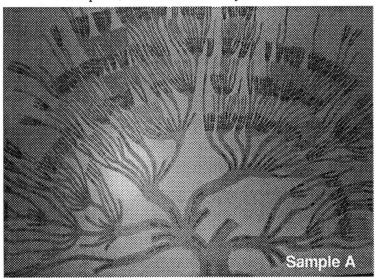

Sample A

plywood, with each person being identified by his given name. One benefit of using plywood is the ability to correct mistakes easier. To ensure the board will last, use grade A plywood or MDO[20] board. Fill the edges with wood putty, sand plywood surfaces. Seal with a water sealer such as Thompson's if it will be stored outside. Paint both sides to minimize warping. Next paint the names using letters approximately three-eighths of an inch high so photographs can be read. Be cautious when lettering: e's, c's, and o's as their centers can often become blobs. Color and media are discussed in the Artist's Palette section.

Another option is the use of a bed-sheet. Its benefit is storage and shipping. Quite a few generations of common names can be represented on a double size sheet with three-eighths inch letters. First wash and iron the bed sheet, then apply the

[20] MDO is a sheet of plywood with a smooth paper surface, excellent for making signs.

color coded names with a liquid embroidery pen. These pens are fairly easy to use, and easily accessible. It takes

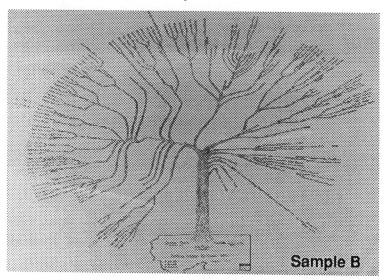

Sample B

approximately six inches per couple, with half-an-inch between names. To keep the generations in a circular format use a string compass. Don't make the generation rings too dark as they may not wash out.

Fix a guest name plaque, even listing on a blackboard is acceptable. Guests want to be acknowledged too.

For single day events the pressure sensitive name tags are fine. Here color coding could identify family branches, current state of residence, or visitors. These tags may harm leather, velvet, velveteen and silk. When name tags are used for numerous activities the safety pin clear plastic name tags are good. Badge-A-Mint[21] buttons encourage standard or custom designing. The design can be developed to indicate prepaid activities and meals through color or art. Teenagers and children can have a delightful time making souvenir name tags.

---

[21] Badge-A-Mint, Box 800, Civic Industrial Park, LaSalle, IL 61301

Permanent engraved name tags are available through specialty advertising representatives, and many stationary stores. Allow three months for the order to be processed.

A large identification sign for the group can be advantageous. Butcher paper banners are inexpensive, short lived, but effective, whereas canvas banners with grommets can be used for many years. It takes the same amount of time to produce quality work either on canvas or butcher paper. Another option is the sandwich sign which is lower to the ground, easily read by pedestrians and movable. Perhaps the easiest overall identification is to have the family look for five feet fluorescent helium filled balloons.

To make a sandwich sign use smooth half-inch smooth plywood, or MDO board. Cut two identical rectangles approximately three-by-five-feet. Prepare for painting as for the family tree. When lettering identical messages, use butcher paper to make a pattern. Either carbonize the back side of the layout by rubbing charcoal or a soft leaded pencil onto the back side of the areas to be transferred, or use carbon paper. Too much charcoal or other gritty residue left on the board after transferring may cause the paint's edges to run. Too little will result in an insufficient transfer. When the paint has dried, connect the rectangles at the top with two hinges. Mount a strap midway on the signs to keep them from opening too far.

Banner fabric is often difficult to find. A good alternative is a tightly woven fabric such as vinyl table cloths. The minimum size is about three-by-ten-feet, unless you plan to span a roadway. Hem the edges and add grommets about every eighteen inches, this allows a rope to be woven through its length. If the material is durable you may get by with grommets only on the ends and pulling the rope taut.

<u>Artist's Palette</u>

Media makes a major difference in the completed project. Tempera is a water soluble, inexpensive paint generally used for poster work. Acrylic is also water soluble and is used in lots of house paint. Satin and glossy finish acrylic paints are more satisfactory in sign work. However, the premium is the sign painter's enamel. It gives a marvelous finish and is sufficient with one application. It is difficult to find in some areas, and more expensive. Marker pens are fine for letters and lines, the same width as the pen. Once applied to paper the ink has a tendency to fade in sunlight, and run when wet.

Tools are another important factor, as good brushes can ensure smooth lines. Lettering brushes are tapered or flat across the bottom. For large signs use a blunt edged brush. Foam brushes are quite satisfactory as the width remains consistent.

Silk screening is a marvelous method to make repeat patterns for reunion T-shirts. It is not difficult, but few families will make their own shirts, if you decide to make your own there are books available at most craft shops and libraries.

Composition is another factor. As your surname will be the primary attraction it should be the dominant factor. This can be achieved by emphasizing the name through use of contrasting color, or bold lettering. Use a pleasant combination of lettering fonts (styles). The layout should reflect the theme of the over-all event. Keep the messages clean, concise and complete.

Many people like Old English and Black German

ABCDEFGHIJKLMNOPQ
RSTUVWXYZ1234567890

lettering which is beautiful, but challenging to letter and difficult to read in large quantities. Basically, there are three types
of lettering; text, Roman or Gothic. These three plus serifs (little

ABCDEFGH
I J KL NMOP
QRS TUVW&
XYZ?$123
4567890¢

CLASSIC ROMAN

feet on the edges of the letters) and those without make
countless variations.

SHADOWS normally fall on the right side.

157

Another major consideration in composition is the spacing of the letters. Optical spacing is when the lettering is more less done by the eye, and looks good. Mechanical spacing is exactly that, precisely placed at a specified distance from surrounding letters. Letters with curves should nestle closer to their neighbors, as should the letter "i."

OPTICAL
SPACING

MECHANICAL
SPACING

Before painting the signs, check the general scenery and locations where the signs are to be placed. To make the signs readily readable they should not merge with the backgrounds.

As a rule painting dark letters on a light backgrounds is faster and easier than painting light colored letters on a dark background. Yellow letters on a black or royal blue, royal blue or red letters on a white have good distance readability.

There is lots of room to be creative, and stimulate others to share in the process of making a ...

..."Thank goodness I came" event.

MECHANICAL
SPACING
OF UNIFORM
LETTERS AND
MARGINS OF
EQUAL WIDTH
MAKE A POSTER
MONOTONOUS

THE EFFECTIVE USE OF
CONTRAST
POWERFUL
HEAD-LINES
WITH THE REST OF THE
COPY ARRANGED IN
SUBORDINATE GROUPS
BALANCED
ON OPTICAL CENTER
·· AND ··
A GENEROUS USE
OF BLANK SPACE
· WITH ·
LIBERAL MARGINS
ARE THE FIRST AIDS
TO A GOOD LAYOUT

FAMILY REUNIONS AND CLAN GATHERINGS

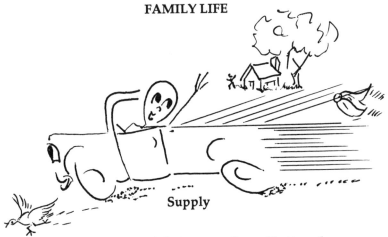

Supply

Some families said their events flowed better when a single person was responsible for gathering borrowing and purchasing necessary items. If you decide to implement this concept ask each of the committees to give you their list of needed material, equipment and other items.

Make a list of what items are available within the family for use at the event; large coffee pots, thermal coolers, etc. Be sure to keep accurate records of who owns what and return within a few weeks of the reunion.

For items that are purchased, many wholesale warehouses sell at a discount, and will accept unopened packages, if returned promptly.

This position should probably be filled by someone living within the reunion area, have a pickup or small truck, and have plenty of time to coordinate.

If the gathering is going to be held on a private ranch or resident this position is most important. Chairs, tables, and other basics must be gathered, prepared for use, cleaned and returned.

If you think of a good method to handle this position, please share it with the rest of us.

cont'd from pg: 105

My Barbecues are the Pits.

from cracking out due to the intense heat during 'firing'. The concrete needs to be well cured before a full-fledged barbecue is planned. A few small fires will help cure the concrete.

Now that the pit is cured, you'll need a few more items to be ready for the big fire. To cover the pit when not being used and during barbecues, I use a four foot by eight foot piece of heavy steel one-eighth inch in thickness.

While barbecuing, place a couple steel fence posts across the pit to support the cover and the sand or dirt used to seal the pit. As for the material used to cover the pit, sand is best since it doesn't pack down and can be used over and over. It also doubles for a sand playground for my kids or can be used around the yard for various projects. I usually get one pick-up load every time I have a barbecue. You'll need enough to cover the top with about ten inches of sand, which will take one-and-one-fourth to one-and-one-half yards.

This just about covers the 'ground work'. I will mention that site selection is important. The starting fire will produce intense heat and flames may reach six to eight feet above the ground level. I've scorched some trees near my pit.

Before we get to the 'meat' of the subject you'll need to know about fuel. It takes lots of wood, about half-a-cord, depending on the size of the wood. I use oak, preferably black oak. Using small diameter limbs less than four inches in diameter will take more wood than if you use large limbs, trunks, or whole stumps. I usually start the fire with some softwood, then go to small diameter limbs, and finally the larger stuff.

Now that the pit is ready we need to get the timing set so everything will be ready when its supposed to be. The fire should be started about eight hours before putting the meat in. It will take about eight to ten hours for the meat to cook, depending on what is on the menu. (We'll get to that later.) For now, figuring backwards from say an eating time of 5:00 P.M. Saturday it takes an hour to get the meat out and ready to serve. Then the meat should be put in at 8:00 A.M. and come out at 4:00 P.M. That means the fire should be started around midnight on Friday.

Oh, I forgot to mention lights and clearing the area so no one trips during the fire preparation. This type of pit is dangerous once fired, so the 'pit crew' should not be celebrating too much. The fire has to be watched fairly close the first couple of hours, till the coals begin to pile up. I generally fill the pit after the first two hours, then retire for about three hours and fill it up again. This will get you three more hours of rest until the meat is to be put in at 8:00 A.M.

Ah yes, the meat! The usual is a half or whole pork. A whole hog, about 150 pounds, would need a full ten hours, since you want it done thoroughly. I've never done a half-of-beef, but I did a large Holstein hind quarters in a little over eight hours, and we had rare, medium, and well-done meat. One new years we barbecued two goats, one young wether, and one old wether. You couldn't tell which was which. It was great.

Whatever meat you choose, make it worthwhile. Serving any less than fifty people is not worth the effort for a pit barbecue, so you'll need at least half a pig, whole goat, or large lamb.

Preparing the meat is basically the same for all meats, just a variation of herbs, spices, and sauces. Lay the meat out on a large table. Dryer type meats could be rubbed down with oil first. Then a coat of your favorite barbecue sauce in liberal portions. Next sprinkle on herbs and spices. I like to cut onions in large chunks and put in the body cavity. For poultry eaters take a few chickens, cornish hens or a turkey and place just inside the ribs - spice them up, too.

You now need a long roll of heavy duty aluminum foil. Roll out several pieces, a foot or so past the ends of the shoulder and rump. Splice these pieces together so they can be wrapped around the meat to completely seal. You may have to cut off or tie down the ends of the legs so they don't rip through the foil. A second layer of foil doesn't hurt anything. Next, get some good clean large burlap bags. You need to get three layers of burlap around the meat. Wet each layer as it is put on. The first two layers may be tied with string. Tie the final layer with wire. I use bailing-wire, of course. Don't use galvanized wire as it will give off toxic fumes when heated. Make two or more loops in the wire for hand holds. Get two-or-three six-to-eight-foot lengths of old telephone wire. I use this because it is very strong, and rigid. Make loops on each end. Now you're ready to carry this to the pit area. Hopefully, you prepared the meat Friday evening before the fire was started. If you didn't and have to prepare it sometime between midnight and 8:00 A.M. you may not have enough strength left to carry it to the pit. Be careful, because the fire should be burned down to two-to-three feet of red hot coals. Tie the telephone wires to the loops of baling wire around the meat. Have two or more people lower the meat onto the coals. Make sure the ends of the lowering wires are well outside the fire area, so they can be found easily when the meat is ready to be removed. Lay a couple steel fence posts across the pit to support the weight of the sand. Now lay the sheet of metal over the opening quickly. Watch your fingers as the heat will be intense at the edge of the cover. Start covering the top with sand and finish this quickly. Make sure there is no smoke escaping and the top of the sand is not real hot; warm is okay.

You should be really pooped by this time. Time for a little nap. You'll have eight-to-ten hours of rest then get ready for the shindig to start. When it is finally ready to take out the meat I find there are more volunteers than shovels to uncover the pit. Carefully remove the last of the sand and get gloves for those that will remove the metal cover. Again the heat will be intense as the cover comes off. Find the lifting wires and carefully lift the meat out. Have a large table ready to set the meat on. Cut the wires off and remove the burlap completely. Cut the foil away and reveal the fruits of your labor. It may be a little crusty but just under this will be some of the best eating you'll ever encounter. The meat usually can't be cut, so I use tongs to serve the tender morsels.

From start to finish, this is a lot of work. Planning needs to be a priority or you'll have a crowd on the verge of rioting. My first attempt resulted in a slightly toasted half-a-pig. Everyone loved it anyway, but I've heard of some nightmares about meat almost rare enough to climb out of the pit without help. But, with patience and preparation you'll have a great tasting piece of meat and your friends will think you're the greatest cook of all time.

Good Luck!

Ross P. Singleton

P.O. Box 1854
Yreka, CA 96097

Dear Fellow Clan Enthusiasts:

It has been a pleasure to compile the examples shared. Most people who organize clan gatherings do so to perpetuate the pride of heritage in their youth, keep the family together, and enrich their own life experience.

A few attendees of clan gatherings said they grit their teeth at the thought of going. When questioned it seems to revolve around social competitiveness, narrow scope of activities and interests available. From their comments we know how ours should be friendly, versatile and stimulating.

Looking forward to hearing your experiences, and what you would recommend to future clan organizers. Some people, during the years, said they would be interested in networking with others clan organizers to continue sharing experiences...and suggested a newsletter. What is your opinion?

Thank you for taking time from your busy schedule to share. Good luck on making your event a "Thank goodness I came" memory!

Sincerely,

Shari

Shari Fiock

BIBLIOGRAPHY

To the best of my knowledge, this is the only book on organizing large family reunions and clan gatherings. In addition to those referred to in "Family Reunions and Clan Gatherings" the following might be beneficial. Remember, though, there are countless books on organization, motivation, writing, design, lettering, cooking and family life available.

COPING WITH DIFFICULT PEOPLE
     BY Robert Branson   Anchor Press/Doubleday

FAMILY FUN OUTDOORS
     BY Russell P. McFall   Crowell   1965

FAMILY GAME BOOK
     BY David A. Boehm   Doubleday   1967

FAMILY TREE: AN ANTHOLOGY ABOUT FAMILY RELATIONSHIPS
     by Johanna Johnstone   World Publishing Co.   1967

HOW TO RUN ANY ORGANIZATION
     BY Theodore Caplon   Holt, Reinhart & Winston

RECRUITING, TRAINING AND MOTIVATING VOLUNTEER WORKERS
     BY Arthur R. Pell   Pilot Books

THE COMPETE BOOK OF GAMES
     BY Clement Wood and Gloria Goddard
                    Doubleday   1940
THE QUICK MOTIVATION METHOD
     BY Thomas Quick   St. Martin's Press

FAMILY REUNIONS AND CLAN GATHERINGS

Index

NOTES:

FAMILY REUNIONS AND CLAN GATHERINGS